The USEFUL PROVERBS

by

Kathy Collard Miller

This Billy Graham Evangelistic Association special edition is published with permission from World Publishing, Inc.

Grand Rapids, Michigan 49418 USA

The Useful Proverbs
Copyright 1997 by Kathy Collard Miller
Published by World Publishing, Inc.
Grand Rapids, Michigan 49418

Half-brackets (⌊ ⌋) enclose words that the translation team supplied because the context contains meaning that is not explicitly stated in the original language.

Produced for World Publishing by The Livingstone Corporation, Carol Stream, IL.
Design and typesetting by Design Corps, Batavia, IL.

ISBN 0-913367-94-X

Printed in the United States of America

Dedication

This book is lovingly dedicated to my friend, Neva B. True. Neva is a woman who has memorized more of the Proverbs than anyone I know. Thank you, Neva, for modeling a godly woman who makes a priority of meditating on Scripture.

Table of Contents

Introduction

How to Use *The Useful Proverbs*

Have you ever been working on a project—Bible study, writing assignment, or speech preparation—and you recall a concept contained in the Book of Proverbs but can't remember the verse or wording? You use a concordance to look up a word that you think is in the verse—but can't find it. You need that verse but become more and more frustrated trying to find it as you flip through the 31 chapters of Proverbs.

The Useful Proverbs is the answer to your dilemma. Within this book you will find every verse of Proverbs included in one or more categories. By turning to a concept title, such as anger, parenting, or humility, you will find at your fingertips verses that refer to such ideas.

The Useful Proverbs can also be used as a devotional guide. You can either concentrate on one category each day reading from front to back or you can pick a particular topic's verses to meditate on based upon your need that day.

I trust that this resource will be a blessing for you.

Kathy Collard Miller

ANGER AND CONFLICT

The circumstances of life can make us so angry! If only things would go the way we want, we wouldn't get aggravated! The Proverbs have some wise things to say about handling those irritating feelings and responses.

Anger and Conflict

Do not quarrel with a person for no reason
  if he has not harmed you.
Do not envy a violent person.
Do not choose any of his ways.

3:30-31

Wicked people cannot sleep
  unless they do wrong,
    and they are robbed of their sleep
      unless they make someone stumble.
        They eat food obtained through wrongdoing
          and drink wine obtained through violence.

4:16-17

Blessings cover the head of a righteous person,
  but violence covers the mouths of wicked people.

10:6

When a stubborn fool is irritated, he shows it immediately,
  but a sensible person hides the insult.

12:16

A person eats well as a result of his speaking ability,
  but the appetite of treacherous people ⌊craves⌋ violence.

13:2

A short-tempered person acts stupidly,
  and a person who plots evil is hated. . . .
A person of great understanding is patient,
  but a short temper is the height of stupidity.
A tranquil heart makes for a healthy body,
  but jealousy is ⌊like⌋ bone cancer.

14:17,29-30

A king is delighted with a servant who acts wisely,
  but he is furious with one who acts shamefully.

14:35

A gentle answer turns away rage,
  but a harsh word stirs up anger. . . .
A hothead stirs up a fight,
  but one who holds his temper calms disputes.

15:1,18

A devious person spreads quarrels.
A gossip separates the closest of friends.
A violent person misleads his neighbor
  and leads him on a path that is not good. . . .
  Better to get angry slowly than to be a hero.
  Better to be even-tempered than to capture a city.

16:28-29,32

Better a bite of dry bread ⌊eaten⌋ in peace
  than a family feast filled with strife.

17:1

Starting a quarrel is ⌊like⌋ opening a floodgate,
  so stop before the argument gets out of control. . . .
Whoever loves sin loves a quarrel.
Whoever builds his city gate high invites destruction. . . .
  Whoever has knowledge controls his words,
    and a person who has understanding is even-tempered.

17:14,19,27

By talking, a fool gets into an argument,
  and his mouth invites a beating.
A fool's mouth is his ruin.
His lips are a trap to his soul. . . .
Flipping a coin ends quarrels
  and settles ⌊issues⌋ between powerful people.
An offended brother is more ⌊resistant⌋ than a strong city,
  and disputes are like the locked gate of a castle tower.

18:6-7,18-19

The stupidity of a person turns his life upside down,
 and his heart rages against the LORD. . . .
A person with good sense is patient,
 and it is to his credit that he overlooks an offense.
The rage of a king is like the roar of a lion,
 but his favor is like dew on the grass. . . .
A person who has a hot temper will pay for it.
 If you rescue him, you will have to do it over and over.

19:3,11-12,19

The rage of a king is like the roar of a lion.
 Whoever makes him angry forfeits his life.
Avoiding a quarrel is honorable.
 After all, any stubborn fool can start a fight. . . .
Do not say, "I'll get even with you!"
 Wait for the LORD, and he will save you.

20:2-3,22

The violence of wicked people will drag them away
 since they refuse to do what is just. . . .
Better to live on a corner of a roof
 than to share a home with a quarreling woman. . . .
A gift ⌊given⌋ in secret calms anger,
 and a secret bribe calms great fury. . . .
Better to live in a desert
 than with a quarreling and angry woman.

21:7,9,14,19

Drive out a mocker, and conflict will leave.
 Quarreling and abuse will stop. . . .
Do not be a friend of one who has a bad temper,
 and never keep company with a hothead,
  or you will learn his ways
   and set a trap for yourself.

22:10,24-25

Do not be happy when your enemy falls,
and do not feel glad when he stumbles.
The LORD will see it, he won't like it,
and he will turn his anger away from that person.

24:17-18

With patience you can persuade a ruler,
and a soft tongue can break bones.

25:15

If your enemy is hungry, give him some food to eat,
and if he is thirsty, give him some water to drink.
⌊In this way⌋ you will make him feel guilty and ashamed,
and the LORD will reward you.

⌊As⌋ the north wind brings rain,
so a whispering tongue brings angry looks.
Better to live on a corner of a roof
than to share a home with a quarreling woman.

25:21-24

⌊Like⌋ grabbing a dog by the ears,
⌊so⌋ is a bystander who gets involved
in someone else's quarrel.
Like a madman who shoots flaming arrows,
arrows, and death,
so is the person who tricks his neighbor
and says, "I was only joking!"

26:17-19

Without wood a fire goes out,
and without gossip a quarrel dies down.
⌊As⌋ charcoal fuels burning coals and wood fuels fire,
so a quarrelsome person fuels a dispute.

26:20-21

A stone is heavy, and sand weighs a lot,
but annoyance caused by a stubborn fool
is heavier than both.
Anger is cruel, and fury is overwhelming,
but who can survive jealousy?

27:3-4

A greedy person stirs up a fight,
but whoever trusts the LORD prospers.

28:25

Mockers create an uproar in a city,
but wise people turn away anger.

When a wise person goes to court with a stubborn fool,
he may rant and rave,
but there is no peace and quiet. . . .
A fool expresses all his emotions,
but a wise person controls them. . . .
An angry person stirs up a fight,
and a hothead does much wrong.

29:8-9,11,22

"Do not slander a slave to his master.
The slave will curse you,
and you will be found guilty."

A certain kind of person curses his father
and does not bless his mother.
A certain kind of person thinks he is pure
but is not washed from his own feces.
A certain kind of person looks around arrogantly
and is conceited.
A certain kind of person,
whose teeth are like swords
and whose jaws are ⌊like⌋ knives,
devours oppressed people from the earth
and people from among humanity.

30:10-14

As churning milk produces butter
and punching a nose produces blood,
so stirring up anger produces a fight.

30:33

AVOIDING SIN

We know we'd be a lot happier if we avoided sin, but it's hard sometimes to resist Satan's pull. It's a good thing we have God's Word to give us instructions for doing the right thing.

Avoiding Sin

Wisdom will come into your heart.
Knowledge will be pleasant to your soul.
Foresight will protect you.
Understanding will guard you.

2:10-11

By mercy and faithfulness, peace is made with the LORD.
By the fear of the LORD, evil is avoided. . . .
The highway of decent people turns away from evil.
Whoever watches his way preserves his own life.

Pride precedes a disaster,
and an arrogant attitude precedes a fall. . . .
A violent person misleads his neighbor
and leads him on a path that is not good.

16:6,17-18,29

A person without knowledge is no good.
A person in a hurry makes mistakes.

19:2

Sensible people foresee trouble and hide ⌊from it⌋,
but gullible people go ahead
and suffer ⌊the consequence⌋. . . .
A devious person has thorns and traps ahead of him.
Whoever guards himself will stay far away from them. . . .
Do not be a friend of one who has a bad temper,
and never keep company with a hothead,
or you will learn his ways
and set a trap for yourself.

22:3,5,24-25

Sensible people foresee trouble and hide.
Gullible people go ahead ⌊and⌋ suffer.

27:12

Blessed is the one who is always fearful ⌊of sin⌋,
but whoever is hard-hearted falls into disaster.

28:14

BAD HABITS AND ADDICTIONS

Life certainly is a challenge. There are numerous things we can become obsessive about. God's Word is a powerful reflective tool as it mirrors back to us the things that can rule over us. God offers us hope and help to overcome addictions.

Bad Habits and Addictions

Wine ⌊makes people⌋ mock,
liquor ⌊makes them⌋ noisy,
and everyone under their influence is unwise.

20:1

Do not associate with those who drink too much wine,
with those who eat too much meat,
because both a drunk and a glutton will become poor.
Drowsiness will dress a person in rags.

23:20-21

Who has trouble?
Who has misery?
Who has quarrels?
Who has a complaint?
Who has wounds for no reason?
Who has bloodshot eyes?
Those who drink glass after glass of wine
and mix it with everything.
Do not look at wine
because it is red,
because it sparkles in the cup,
because it goes down smoothly.
Later it bites like a snake
and strikes like a poisonous snake.
Your eyes will see strange sights,
and your mouth will say embarrassing things.
You will be like someone lying down
in the middle of the sea
or like someone lying down on top
of a ship's mast, saying,
"They strike me, but I feel no pain.
They beat me, but I'm not aware of it.
Whenever I wake up,
I'm going to look for another drink."

23:29-35

When you find honey, eat only as much as you need.
  Otherwise, you will have too much and vomit.

25:16

One who is full despises honey,
  but to one who is hungry,
    even bitter food tastes sweet. . . .
Hell and decay are never satisfied,
  and a person's eyes are never satisfied.

27:7,20

"What, my son?
What, son to whom I gave birth?
What, son of my prayers?
  Don't give your strength to women
    or your power to those who ruin kings.

"It is not for kings, Lemuel.
It is not for kings to drink wine or for rulers to crave liquor.
  Otherwise, they drink and forget what they have decreed
    and change the standard of justice
      for all oppressed people.
Give liquor to a person who is dying
  and wine to one who feels resentful.
    Such a person drinks
      and forgets his poverty
        and does not remember his trouble anymore.

"Speak out for the one who cannot speak,
  for the rights of those who are doomed.
Speak out,
  judge fairly,
    and defend the rights of oppressed and needy people."

31:1-9

COMMUNICATION

The tongue can be a blessing or a curse. Often we say things before realizing their consequences. These Proverbs give us plenty to think about—before we open our mouths.

Remove dishonesty from your mouth.
Put deceptive speech far away from your lips.

4:24

A good-for-nothing scoundrel is a person
who has a dishonest mouth.
He winks his eye,
makes a signal with his foot,
⌊and⌋ points with his fingers.
He devises evil all the time with a twisted mind.
He spreads conflict.
That is why disaster will come on him suddenly.
In a moment he will be crushed beyond recovery.

6:12-15

There are six things that the LORD hates,
even seven that are disgusting to him:
arrogant eyes,
a lying tongue,
hands that kill innocent people,
a mind devising wicked plans,
feet that are quick to do wrong,
a dishonest witness spitting out lies,
and a person who spreads conflict among relatives.

6:16-19

The one who is truly wise accepts commands,
but the one who talks foolishly
will be thrown down headfirst. . . .
Whoever winks with his eye causes heartache.
The one who talks foolishly will be thrown down headfirst.
The mouth of a righteous person is a fountain of life,
but the mouths of wicked people conceal violence.

10:8,10-11

Wisdom is found on the lips of a person who has understanding,
but a rod is for the back of one without sense.
Those who are wise store up knowledge,
but the mouth of a stubborn fool invites ruin.

10:13-14

Sin is unavoidable when there is much talk,
but whoever seals his lips is wise.
The tongue of a righteous person is pure silver.
The hearts of wicked people are worthless.
The lips of a righteous person feed many,
but stubborn fools die because they have no sense. . . .
The mouth of a righteous person increases wisdom,
but a devious tongue will be cut off.
The lips of a righteous person announce good will,
but the mouths of wicked people are devious.

10:19-21,31-32

With his talk a godless person can ruin his neighbor,
but righteous people are rescued by knowledge. . . .
With the blessing of decent people a city is raised up,
but by the words of wicked people, it is torn down.

A person who despises a neighbor has no sense,
but a person who has understanding keeps quiet.

11:9,11-12

The words of wicked people are a deadly ambush,
but the words of decent people rescue. . . .
An evil person is trapped by his own sinful talk,
but a righteous person escapes from trouble.
One person enjoys good things as a result of his speaking ability.
Another is paid according to what his hands have accomplished.

12:6,13-14

Communication

A truthful witness speaks honestly,
but a lying witness speaks deceitfully.
Careless words stab like a sword,
but the words of wise people bring healing.
The word of truth lasts forever,
but lies last only a moment.
Deceit is in the heart of those who plan evil,
but joy belongs to those who advise peace.

12:17-20

Lips that lie are disgusting to the LORD,
but honest people are his delight. . . .
A person's anxiety will weigh him down,
but an encouraging word makes him joyful.

12:22,25

A person eats well as a result of his speaking ability,
but the appetite of treacherous people ⌊craves⌋ violence.
Whoever controls his mouth protects his own life.
Whoever has a big mouth comes to ruin. . . .
The teachings of a wise person are a fountain of life
to turn ⌊one⌋ away from the grasp of death.

13:2-3,14

Because of a stubborn fool's words a whip is lifted against him,
but wise people are protected by their speech. . . .
In hard work there is always something gained,
but idle talk leads only to poverty.

14:3,23

A gentle answer turns away rage,
but a harsh word stirs up anger.
The tongues of wise people give good expression to knowledge,
but the mouths of fools pour out a flood of stupidity. . . .
A soothing tongue is a tree of life,
but a deceitful tongue breaks the spirit.

15:1-2,4

The lips of wise people spread knowledge,
but a foolish attitude does not. . . .
The mind of a person who has understanding
searches for knowledge,
but the mouths of fools feed on stupidity. . . .
A person is delighted to hear an answer from his own mouth,
and a timely word—oh, how good!

15:7,14,23

The thoughts of evil people are disgusting to the LORD,
but pleasant words are pure to him. . . .
The heart of a righteous person carefully considers
how to answer,
but the mouths of wicked people pour out
a flood of evil things.

15:26,28

The plans of the heart belong to humans,
but an answer on the tongue comes from the LORD. . . .
The person who is truly wise is called understanding,
and speaking sweetly helps others learn. . . .
A wise person's heart controls his speech,
and what he says helps others learn.
Pleasant words are ⌊like⌋ honey from a honeycomb—
sweet to the spirit and healthy for the body.

16:1,21,23-24

A worthless person plots trouble,
and his speech is like a burning fire.
A devious person spreads quarrels.
A gossip separates the closest of friends.
A violent person misleads his neighbor
and leads him on a path that is not good.
Whoever winks his eye is plotting something devious.
Whoever bites his lips has finished his evil work.

16:27-30

Communication

An evildoer pays attention to wicked lips.
A liar opens his ears to a slanderous tongue.
Whoever makes fun of a poor person insults his maker.
Whoever is happy ⌊to see someone's⌋ distress
will not escape punishment. . . .
Whoever forgives an offense seeks love,
but whoever keeps bringing up the issue
separates the closest of friends.

17:4-5,9

Starting a quarrel is ⌊like⌋ opening a floodgate,
so stop before the argument gets out of control. . . .
Whoever loves sin loves a quarrel.
Whoever builds his city gate high invites destruction.
A twisted mind never finds happiness,
and one with a devious tongue ⌊repeatedly⌋ gets into trouble.

17:14,19-20

Whoever has knowledge controls his words,
and a person who has understanding is even-tempered.

Even a stubborn fool is thought to be wise if he keeps silent.
He is considered intelligent if he keeps his lips sealed.

17:27-28

A fool does not find joy in understanding
but only in expressing his own opinion.

When wickedness comes, contempt also comes,
and insult comes along with disgrace.
The words of a person's mouth are like deep waters.
The fountain of wisdom is an overflowing stream.

18:2-4

By talking, a fool gets into an argument,
and his mouth invites a beating.
A fool's mouth is his ruin.
His lips are a trap to his soul.

18:6-7

Whoever gives an answer before he listens
is stupid and shameful.

18:13

A person's speaking ability provides for his stomach.
His talking provides him a living.
The tongue has the power of life and death,
and those who love to talk will have to eat their own words.

18:20-21

A poor person is timid when begging,
but a rich person is blunt when replying.

18:23

There are gold and plenty of jewels,
but the lips of knowledge are precious gems. . . .
Whoever goes around as a gossip tells secrets.
Do not associate with a person whose mouth is always open.

20:15,19

Whoever guards his mouth and his tongue
keeps himself out of trouble.

21:23

Whoever loves a pure heart and whoever speaks graciously
has a king as his friend.
The LORD's eyes watch over knowledge,
but he overturns the words of a treacherous person.

22:11-12

Open your ears, and hear the words of wise people,
and set your mind on the knowledge I give you.
It is pleasant if you keep them in mind
⌊so that⌋ they will be on the tip of your tongue,
so that your trust may be in the LORD.
Today I have made them known to you, especially to you.

22:17-19

Communication

Do not talk directly to a fool,
because he will despise the wisdom of your words.
23:9

My son,
if you have a wise heart,
my heart will rejoice as well.
My heart rejoices when you speak what is right.
23:15-16

Do not envy evil people
or wish you were with them,
because their minds plot violence,
and their lips talk trouble.
24:1-2

Matters of wisdom are beyond the grasp of a stubborn fool.
At the city gate he does not open his mouth.
24:7

⌊Like⌋ golden apples in silver settings,
⌊so⌋ is a word spoken at the right time.
⌊Like⌋ a gold ring and a fine gold ornament,
⌊so⌋ is constructive criticism to the ear of one who listens.
Like the coolness of snow on a harvest day,
⌊so⌋ is a trustworthy messenger to those who send him:
He refreshes his masters.
⌊Like⌋ a dense fog or a dust storm,
⌊so⌋ is a person who brags about a gift that he does not give.

With patience you can persuade a ruler,
and a soft tongue can break bones.
25:11-15

⌊Like⌋ a club and a sword and a sharp arrow,
⌊so⌋ is a person who gives false testimony
against his neighbor.
25:18

⌊Like⌋ taking off a coat on a cold day
or pouring vinegar on baking soda,
so is singing songs to one who has an evil heart. . . .
⌊Like⌋ cold water to a thirsty soul,
so is good news from far away.

25:20,25

Like a fluttering sparrow,
like a darting swallow,
so a hastily spoken curse does not come to rest. . . .
Do not answer a fool with his own stupidity,
or you will be like him.
Answer a fool with his own stupidity,
or he will think he is wise.
Whoever uses a fool to send a message
cuts off his own feet and brings violence upon himself.

26:2,4-6

⌊Like⌋ a lame person's limp legs,
so is a proverb in the mouths of fools.

26:7

⌊Like⌋ a thorn stuck in a drunk's hand,
so is a proverb in the mouths of fools. . . .
Like a madman who shoots flaming arrows, arrows, and death,
so is the person who tricks his neighbor
and says, "I was only joking!"

26:9,18-19

⌊As⌋ charcoal fuels burning coals and wood fuels fire,
so a quarrelsome person fuels a dispute.

26:21

⌊Like⌋ a clay pot covered with cheap silver,
⌊so⌋ is smooth talk that covers up an evil heart.
Whoever is filled with hate disguises it with his speech,
but inside he holds on to deceit.

When he talks charmingly, do not trust him
because of the seven disgusting things in his heart.
His hatred is deceitfully hidden,
but his wickedness will be revealed to the community.

26:23-26

Do not brag about tomorrow,
because you do not know what another day may bring.
Praise should come from another person
and not from your own mouth,
from a stranger and not from your own lips. . . .
Open criticism is better than unexpressed love.

27:1-2,5

Whoever blesses his friend early in the morning
with a loud voice—
his blessing is considered a curse.

27:14

The crucible is for refining silver and the smelter for gold,
but a person ⌊is tested⌋ by the praise given to him.

27:21

Whoever criticizes people will be
more highly regarded in the future
than the one who flatters with his tongue.

28:23

A person who flatters his neighbor
is spreading a net for him to step into.

29:5

Have you met a person who is quick to answer?
There is more hope for a fool than for him.

29:20

Every word of God has proven to be true.
He is a shield to those who come to him for protection.
Do not add to his words,
or he will reprimand you, and you will be found to be a liar.
30:5-6

A certain kind of person,
whose teeth are like swords
and whose jaws are ⌊like⌋ knives,
devours oppressed people from the earth
and people from among humanity.
30:14

Speak out for the one who cannot speak,
for the rights of those who are doomed.
Speak out,
judge fairly,
and defend the rights of oppressed and needy people.
31:8-9

She speaks with wisdom,
and on her tongue there is tender instruction. . . .
Charm is deceptive, and beauty evaporates,
⌊but⌋ a woman who has the fear of the LORD
should be praised.
Reward her for what she has done,
and let her achievements praise her at the city gates.
31:26,30-31

DISCIPLINE, CORRECTION, AND INSTRUCTION

None of us like or invite criticism, yet we know receiving God's reproof and the rebuke of others can be beneficial. These Proverbs encourage us to see the value of such painful interaction.

Discipline, Correction, and Instruction

Wisdom sings her song in the streets.
In the public squares she raises her voice.
At the corners of noisy streets she calls out.
At the entrances to the city she speaks her words, . . .
"Turn to me when I warn you.
I will generously pour out my spirit for you.
I will make my words known to you.

"I called, and you refused to listen.
I stretched out my hands to you,
and no one paid attention.
You ignored all my advice.
You did not want me to warn you. . . .
They refused my advice.
They despised my every warning.
They will eat the fruit of their lifestyle.
They will be stuffed with their own schemes."

1:20-21,23-25,30-31

Do not reject the discipline of the LORD, my son,
and do not resent his warning,
because the LORD warns the one he loves,
even as a father warns a son
with whom he is pleased.

3:11-12

Sons,
listen to ⌊your⌋ father's discipline,
and pay attention in order to gain understanding.
After all, I have taught you well.
Do not abandon my teachings.
When I was a boy ⌊learning⌋ from my father,
when I was a tender and only child of my mother,
they used to teach me and say to me,
"Cling to my words wholeheartedly.
Obey my commands so that you may live.
Acquire wisdom.

Acquire understanding.
Do not forget.
Do not turn away from the words that I have spoken.
Do not abandon wisdom, and it will watch over you.
Love wisdom, and it will protect you.
The beginning of wisdom is to acquire wisdom.
  Acquire understanding with all that you have.
  Cherish wisdom.
    It will raise you up.
    It will bring you honor when you embrace it.
    It will give you a graceful garland for your head.
    It will hand you a beautiful crown."

4:1-9

Cling to discipline.
  Do not relax your grip on it.
    Keep it because it is your life.
Do not stray onto the path of wicked people.
Do not walk in the way of evil people.
  Avoid it.
    Do not walk near it.
      Turn away from it,
        and keep on walking.

4:13-15

My son,
  pay attention to my words.
  Open your ears to what I say.
  Do not lose sight of these things.
  Keep them deep within your heart
    because they are life to those who find them
      and they heal the whole body.
  Guard your heart more than anything else,
    because the source of your life flows from it.

4:20-23

But now, sons,
listen to me,
and do not turn away from what I say to you.
Stay far away from her.
Do not even go near her door.
Either you will surrender your reputation to others
and ⌊the rest of⌋ your years to some cruel person,
or strangers will benefit from your strength
and you will have to work hard in a pagan's house.
Then you will groan when your end comes,
when your body and flesh are consumed.
You will say,
"Oh, how I hated discipline!
How my heart despised correction!
I didn't listen to what my teachers said to me,
nor did I keep my ear open to my instructors.
I almost reached total ruin
in the assembly and in the congregation."

5:7-14

Because the command is a lamp,
the teachings are a light,
and the warnings from discipline are the path of life.

6:23

Whoever corrects a mocker receives abuse.
Whoever warns a wicked person gets hurt.
Do not warn a mocker, or he will hate you.
Warn a wise person, and he will love you.
Give ⌊advice⌋ to a wise person,
and he will become even wiser.
Teach a righteous person,
and he will learn more.

The fear of the LORD is the beginning of wisdom.
The knowledge of the Holy One is understanding.

You will live longer because of me,
   and years will be added to your life.
If you are wise, your wisdom will help you.
If you mock, you alone will be held responsible.

9:7-12

The one who is truly wise accepts commands,
   but the one who talks foolishly
      will be thrown down headfirst. . . .
Wisdom is found on the lips of a person who has understanding,
   but a rod is for the back of one without sense. . . .
Whoever practices discipline is on the way to life,
   but whoever ignores a warning strays.

10:8,13,17

Whoever loves discipline loves to learn,
   but whoever hates correction is a dumb animal.

12:1

A wise son listens to his father's discipline,
   but a mocker does not listen to reprimands. . . .
Whoever refuses to spank his son hates him,
   but whoever loves his son disciplines him from early on.

13:1,24

Arrogance produces only quarreling,
   but those who take advice gain wisdom.

13:10

Whoever despises ⌊God's⌋ words will pay the penalty,
   but the one who fears ⌊God's⌋ commands will be rewarded.

The teachings of a wise person are a fountain of life
   to turn ⌊one⌋ away from the grasp of death. . . .
Poverty and shame come to a person who ignores discipline,
   but whoever pays attention to constructive criticism
      will be honored.

13:13-14,18

A stubborn fool despises his father's discipline,
but whoever appreciates a warning shows good sense. . . .
Discipline is a terrible ⌊burden⌋ to anyone
who leaves the ⌊right⌋ path.
Anyone who hates a warning will die. . . .
A mocker does not appreciate a warning.
He will not go to wise people.

15:5,10,12

The ear that listens to a life-giving warning
will be at home among wise people.

Whoever ignores discipline despises himself,
but the person who listens to warning gains understanding.
The fear of the LORD is discipline ⌊leading to⌋ wisdom,
and humility comes before honor.

15:31-33

The person who is truly wise is called understanding,
and speaking sweetly helps others learn.
Understanding is a fountain of life to the one who has it,
but stubborn fools punish themselves with their stupidity.

16:21-22

The crucible is for refining silver and the smelter for gold,
but the one who purifies hearts ⌊by fire⌋ is the LORD. . . .
A reprimand impresses a person who has understanding
more than a hundred lashes impress a fool.

17:3,10

A loner is out to get what he wants for himself.
He opposes all sound reasoning.
A fool does not find joy in understanding
but only in expressing his own opinion.

18:1-2

The stupidity of a person turns his life upside down,
  and his heart rages against the LORD.

19:3

Listen to advice and accept discipline
  so that you may be wise the rest of your life. . . .
Strike a mocker, and a gullible person may learn a lesson.
  Warn an understanding person,
    and he will gain more knowledge. . . .
If you stop listening to instruction, my son,
  you will stray from the words of knowledge. . . .
Punishments are set for mockers
  and beatings for the backs of fools.

19:20,25,27,29

A person's soul is the LORD's lamp.
  It searches his entire innermost being.

20:27

Brutal beatings cleanse away wickedness.
Such beatings cleanse the innermost being.

20:30

When a mocker is punished, a gullible person becomes wise,
  and when a wise person is instructed, he gains knowledge.

21:11

A righteous person wisely considers the house of a wicked person.
  He throws wicked people into disasters.

21:12

Live a more disciplined life,
  and listen carefully to words of knowledge.
Do not hesitate to discipline a child.
  If you spank him, he will not die.
    Spank him yourself,
      and you will save his soul from hell.

23:12-14

⌊Like⌋ golden apples in silver settings,
⌊so⌋ is a word spoken at the right time.
⌊Like⌋ a gold ring and a fine gold ornament,
⌊so⌋ is constructive criticism to the ear of one who listens.

25:11-12

A whip is for the horse,
a bridle is for the donkey,
and a rod is for the backs of fools.

Do not answer a fool with his own stupidity,
or you will be like him.
Answer a fool with his own stupidity,
or he will think he is wise. . . .
⌊Like⌋ grabbing a dog by the ears,
⌊so⌋ is a bystander who gets involved in someone else's quarrel.

26:3-5,17

Open criticism is better than unexpressed love.
Wounds made by a friend are intended to help,
but an enemy's kisses are too much to bear. . . .
Perfume and incense make the heart glad,
but the sweetness of a friend is a fragrant forest.

27:5-6,9

⌊As⌋ iron sharpens iron,
so one person sharpens the wits of another. . . .
The crucible is for refining silver and the smelter for gold,
but a person ⌊is tested⌋ by the praise given to him.

27:17,21

If you crush a stubborn fool in a mortar with a pestle
along with grain,
⌊even then⌋ his stupidity will not leave him.

27:22

Whoever criticizes people will be
more highly regarded in the future
than the one who flatters with his tongue.

28:23

A person who will not bend after many warnings
will suddenly be broken beyond repair.

29:1

A spanking and a warning produce wisdom,
but an undisciplined child disgraces his mother. . . .
Correct your son, and he will give you peace of mind.
He will bring delight to your soul.

29:15,17

A slave cannot be disciplined with words.
He will not respond, though he may understand. . . .
Pamper a slave from childhood,
and later he will be ungrateful.

29:19,21

Every word of God has proven to be true.
He is a shield to those who come to him for protection.
Do not add to his words,
or he will reprimand you, and you will be found to be a liar.

30:5-6

DISGUSTING THINGS TO GOD

God is holy. Because he is perfect and holy, our sin displeases him. This section names some of those sinful things. How grateful we can be that God sent his Son Jesus to die for us so that we can become acceptable to him.

Disgusting Things to God

The devious person is disgusting to the LORD.
The LORD's intimate advice is with decent people.

3:32

There are six things that the LORD hates,
even seven that are disgusting to him:
arrogant eyes,
a lying tongue,
hands that kill innocent people,
a mind devising wicked plans,
feet that are quick to do wrong,
a dishonest witness spitting out lies,
and a person who spreads conflict among relatives.

6:16-19

Dishonest scales are disgusting to the LORD,
but accurate weights are pleasing to him. . . .
Devious people are disgusting to the LORD,
but he is delighted with those whose ways are innocent.

11:1,20

Lips that lie are disgusting to the LORD,
but honest people are his delight.

12:22

A sacrifice brought by wicked people is disgusting to the LORD,
but the prayers of decent people please him.
The way of wicked people is disgusting to the LORD,
but he loves those who pursue righteousness. . . .
The thoughts of evil people are disgusting to the LORD,
but pleasant words are pure to him.

15:8-9,26

Everyone with a conceited heart is disgusting to the LORD.
    Certainly, ⌊such a person⌋ will not go unpunished. . . .
Wrongdoing is disgusting to kings
    because a throne is established through righteousness.

16:5,12

Whoever approves of wicked people
    and whoever condemns righteous people
        is disgusting to the LORD.

17:15

A double standard of weights and measures—
    both are disgusting to the LORD. . . .
A double standard of weights is disgusting to the LORD,
    and dishonest scales are no good.

20:10,23

The sacrifice of wicked people is disgusting,
    especially if they bring it with evil intent.

21:27

EMPLOYMENT

Since Adam began working in the garden, we've been destined to have jobs. The Scriptures have important advice about vocations. Whether an employee or employer, these Proverbs can help make our jobs less stressful.

Employment

Lazy hands bring poverty,
but hard-working hands bring riches.
Whoever gathers in the summer is a wise son.
Whoever sleeps at harvest time brings shame.

10:4-5

A lazy person craves food and there is none,
but the appetite of hard-working people is satisfied.

13:4

A laborer's appetite works to his advantage,
because his hunger drives him on.

16:26

Do you see a person who is efficient in his work?
He will serve kings.
He will not serve unknown people.

22:29

Do not wear yourself out getting rich.
Be smart enough to stop.
Will you catch only a fleeting glimpse of wealth
before it is gone?
It makes wings for itself like an eagle flying into the sky.

23:4-5

⌊Like⌋ many people who destroy everything,
so is one who hires fools or drifters.

26:10

Whoever takes care of a fig tree can eat its fruit,
and whoever protects his master is honored.

27:18

Be fully aware of the condition of your flock,
and pay close attention to your herds.
Wealth is not forever.
Nor does a crown last from one generation to the next.

⌊When⌋ grass is cut short, the tender growth appears,
and vegetables are gathered on the hills.
Lambs ⌊will provide⌋ you with clothing,
and the money from the male goats will buy a field.
There will be enough goat milk to feed you,
to feed your family,
and to keep your servant girls alive.

27:23-27

A slave cannot be disciplined with words.
He will not respond, though he may understand. . . .
Pamper a slave from childhood,
and later he will be ungrateful.

29:19,21

Do not slander a slave to his master.
The slave will curse you,
and you will be found guilty.

30:10

She wakes up while it is still dark
and gives food to her family
and portions of food to her female slaves.

She picks out a field and buys it.
She plants a vineyard from the profits she has earned.
She puts on strength like a belt
and goes to work with energy.
She sees that she is making a good profit.
Her lamp burns late at night. . . .
She makes linen garments and sells them
and delivers belts to the merchants.
Her children and her husband
stand up and bless her.
In addition, he sings her praises, by saying,
'Many women have done noble work,
but you have surpassed them all!'

31:15-18,24,28-29

FINANCIAL MATTERS

The verses in this section instruct us to maintain the right perspective about wealth. We know God is much more important than how much money we have, so we need a reminder to put him first.

Financial Matters

Honor the LORD with your wealth
  and with the first and best part of all your income.
    Then your barns will be full,
      and your vats will overflow with fresh wine.

3:9-10

Blessed is the one who finds wisdom
  and the one who obtains understanding.
    The profit ⌊gained⌋ from ⌊wisdom⌋ is greater than
      the profit ⌊gained⌋ from silver.
        Its yield is better than fine gold.
⌊Wisdom⌋ is more precious than jewels,
  and all your desires cannot equal it.

3:13-15

My son,
  if you guarantee a loan for your neighbor
    or pledge yourself for a stranger with a handshake,
      you are trapped by the words of your own mouth,
        caught by your own promise.

  Do the following things, my son,
      so that you may free yourself,
    because you have fallen into your neighbor's hands:
      Humble yourself,
        and pester your neighbor.
      Don't let your eyes rest
        or your eyelids close.
      Free yourself like a gazelle from the hand of a hunter
        and like a bird from the hand of a hunter.
Consider the ant, you lazy bum.
Watch its ways, and become wise.
  Although it has no overseer, officer, or ruler,
    in summertime it stores its food supply.
    At harvest time it gathers its food.

How long will you lie there, you lazy bum?
When will you get up from your sleep?

"Just a little sleep,
just a little slumber,
just a little nap."
Then your poverty will come ⌊to you⌋ like a drifter,
and your need will come ⌊to you⌋ like a bandit.

6:1-11

Take my discipline, not silver,
and my knowledge rather than fine gold,
because wisdom is better than jewels.
Nothing you desire can equal it.

8:10-11

Treasures gained dishonestly profit no one,
but righteousness rescues from death.
The LORD will not allow a righteous person to starve,
but he intentionally ignores the desires of a wicked person.

Lazy hands bring poverty,
but hard-working hands bring riches.
Whoever gathers in the summer is a wise son.
Whoever sleeps at harvest time brings shame.

10:2-5

The rich person's wealth is ⌊his⌋ strong city.
Poverty ruins the poor. . . .
It is the LORD's blessing that makes a person rich,
and hard work adds nothing to it.

10:15,22

Riches are of no help on the day of fury,
but righteousness saves from death. . . .
Decent people are saved by their righteousness,
but treacherous people are trapped by their own greed.

11:4,6

Financial Matters

Whoever guarantees a stranger's loan will get into trouble,
but whoever hates the closing of a deal remains secure.
A gracious woman wins respect,
but ruthless men gain riches. . . .
A wicked person earns dishonest wages,
but whoever spreads righteousness earns honest pay.
11:15-16,18

One person spends freely and yet grows richer,
while another holds back what he owes and yet grows poorer.
A generous person will be made rich,
and whoever satisfies others will himself be satisfied.
People will curse the one who hoards grain,
but a blessing will be upon the head of the one
who sells it. . . .
Whoever trusts his riches will fall,
but righteous people will flourish like a green leaf.
11:24-26,28

Whoever works his land will have plenty to eat,
but the one who chases unrealistic dreams has no sense.
12:11

One person pretends to be rich but has nothing.
Another pretends to be poor but has great wealth.
A person's riches are the ransom for his life,
but the poor person does not pay attention to threats. . . .
Wealth ⌊gained⌋ through injustice dwindles away,
but whoever gathers little by little has plenty.
13:7-8,11

Poverty and shame come to a person who ignores discipline,
but whoever pays attention to constructive criticism
will be honored. . . .
Disaster hunts down sinners,
but righteous people are rewarded with good.

Good people leave an inheritance to their grandchildren,
but the wealth of sinners is stored away
for a righteous person.

13:18,21-22

Where there are no cattle, the feeding trough is empty,
but the strength of an ox produces plentiful harvests. . . .
A poor person is hated even by his neighbor,
but a rich person is loved by many.
Whoever despises his neighbor sins,
but blessed is the one who is kind to humble people.

14:4,20-21

In hard work there is always something gained,
but idle talk leads only to poverty.
The crown of wise people is their wealth.
The stupidity of fools is just that—stupidity! . . .
Whoever oppresses the poor insults his maker,
but whoever is kind to the needy honors him.

14:23-24,31

Great treasure is in the house of a righteous person,
but trouble comes along with the income
of a wicked person. . . .
Better to have a little with the fear of the LORD
than great treasure and turmoil.
Better to have a dish of vegetables where there is love
than juicy steaks where there is hate.

15:6,16-17

The LORD tears down the house of an arrogant person,
but he protects the property of widows. . . .
Whoever is greedy for unjust gain brings trouble to his family,
but whoever hates bribes will live.

15:25,27

Better a few ⌊possessions⌋ gained honestly
than many gained through injustice. . . .
Honest balances and scales belong to the LORD.
He made the entire set of weights. . . .
How much better it is to gain wisdom than gold,
and the gaining of understanding
should be chosen over silver.

16:8,11,16

A wise slave will become master over a son who acts shamefully,
and he will share the inheritance with the brothers. . . .
Whoever makes fun of a poor person insults his maker.
Whoever is happy ⌊to see someone's⌋ distress
will not escape punishment.

17:2,5

Why should a fool have money in his hand to buy wisdom
when he doesn't have a mind to grasp anything?

17:16

A person without good sense closes a deal with a handshake.
He guarantees a loan in the presence of his friend. . . .
A wicked person secretly accepts a bribe
to corrupt the ways of justice.

17:18,23

A rich person's wealth is his strong city
and is like a high wall in his imagination. . . .
A gift opens doors for the one who gives it
and brings him into the presence of great people. . . .
A poor person is timid when begging,
but a rich person is blunt when replying.

18:11,16,23

Better to be a poor person who lives innocently
than to be one who talks dishonestly and is a fool. . . .

Wealth adds many friends,
  but a poor person is separated from his friend. . . .
  Many try to win the kindness of a generous person,
    and everyone is a friend to a person who gives gifts.
  The entire family of a poor person hates him.
    How much more do his friends
        keep their distance from him!
      When he chases them with words, they are gone.

19:1,4,6-7

Whoever has pity on the poor lends to the LORD,
  and he will repay him for his good deed.

19:17

Hold on to the garment of one
    who guarantees a stranger's loan,
  and hold responsible the person
      who makes a loan on behalf of a foreigner. . . .
An inheritance quickly obtained in the beginning
  will never be blessed in the end.

20:16,21

The plans of a hard-working person lead to prosperity,
  but everyone who is ⌊always⌋ in a hurry ends up in poverty.
Those who gather wealth by lying are wasting time.
  They are looking for death. . . .
Whoever shuts his ear to the cry of the poor
    will call and not be answered.

21:5-6,13

Whoever loves pleasure will become poor.
Whoever loves wine and expensive food
    will not become rich. . . .
Costly treasure and wealth are in the home of a wise person,
  but a fool devours them.

21:17,20

The desire of a lazy person will kill him
because his hands refuse to work.
All day long he feels greedy,
but a righteous person gives and does not hold back.

21:25-26

A good name is more desirable than great wealth.
Respect is better than silver or gold.
The rich and the poor have this in common:
the LORD is the maker of them all. . . .
On the heels of humility (the fear of the LORD)
are riches and honor and life.

22:1-2,4

A rich person rules poor people,
and a borrower is a slave to a lender. . . .
Whoever is generous will be blessed
because he has shared his food with the poor. . . .
Oppressing the poor for profit
⌊or⌋ giving to the rich
certainly leads to poverty.

22:7,9,16

Do not rob the poor because they are poor
or trample on the rights of an oppressed person
at the city gate,
because the LORD will plead their case
and will take the lives of those who rob them.

22:22-23

Do not be ⌊found⌋ among those who make deals
with a handshake,
among those who guarantee other people's loans.
If you have no money to pay back a loan,
why should your bed be repossessed?

22:26-27

Do not wear yourself out getting rich.
Be smart enough to stop.
  Will you catch only a fleeting glimpse of wealth
    before it is gone?
  It makes wings for itself like an eagle flying into the sky.

23:4-5

Do not move an ancient boundary marker
  or enter fields that belong to orphans,
    because the one who is responsible for them is strong.
      He will plead their case against you.

23:10-11

Do not associate with those who drink too much wine,
  with those who eat too much meat,
    because both a drunk and a glutton will become poor.
      Drowsiness will dress a person in rags.

23:20-21

Buy truth (and do not sell it),
  ⌊that is,⌋ buy wisdom, discipline, and understanding.

23:23

With wisdom a house is built.
With understanding it is established.
With knowledge its rooms are filled
  with every kind of riches, both precious and pleasant.

24:3-4

I passed by a lazy person's field,
  the vineyard belonging to a person without sense.
I saw that it was all overgrown with thistles.
  The ground was covered with weeds,
    and its stone fence was torn down.
When I observed ⌊this⌋, I took it to heart.
I saw it and learned my lesson.

"Just a little sleep,
just a little slumber,
just a little nap."
Then your poverty will come like a drifter,
and your need will come like a bandit.

24:30-34

One who is full despises honey,
but to one who is hungry,
even bitter food tastes sweet.

27:7

Hold on to the garment of one
who guarantees a stranger's loan,
and hold responsible the person
who makes a loan in behalf of a foreigner. . . .
Hell and decay are never satisfied,
and a person's eyes are never satisfied.

27:13,20

Be fully aware of the condition of your flock,
and pay close attention to your herds.
Wealth is not forever.
Nor does a crown last from one generation to the next.

⌊When⌋ grass is cut short, the tender growth appears,
and vegetables are gathered on the hills.
Lambs ⌊will provide⌋ you with clothing,
and the money from the male goats will buy a field.
There will be enough goat milk to feed you,
to feed your family,
and to keep your servant girls alive.

27:23-27

A poor person who oppresses poorer people
is like a driving rain that leaves no food. . . .

Better to be a poor person who has integrity
than to be rich and double-dealing. . . .
Whoever becomes wealthy through ⌊unfair⌋ loans and interest
collects them for the one who is kind to the poor. . . .

28:3,6,8

A rich person is wise in his own eyes,
but a poor person with understanding
sees right through him.

28:11

Whoever works his land will have plenty to eat.
Whoever chases unrealistic dreams
will have plenty of nothing.

A trustworthy person has many blessings,
but anyone in a hurry to get rich
will not escape punishment. . . .
A stingy person is in a hurry to get rich,
not realizing that poverty is about to overtake him. . . .

28:19-20,22

A greedy person stirs up a fight,
but whoever trusts the LORD prospers. . . .
Whoever gives to the poor lacks nothing.
Whoever ignores the poor receives many curses.

28:25,27

A person who loves wisdom makes his father happy,
but one who pays prostitutes wastes his wealth. . . .
A righteous person knows the just cause of the poor.
A wicked person does not understand this. . . .
A poor person and an oppressor have this in common:
The LORD gives both of them sight.
When a king judges the poor with honesty,
his throne will always be secure.

29:3,7,13-14

I've asked you for two things.
Don't keep them from me before I die:
Keep vanity and lies far away from me.
Don't give me either poverty or riches.
Feed me ⌊only⌋ the food I need,
or I may feel satisfied and deny you
and say, 'Who is the LORD?'
or I may become poor and steal
and give the name of my God a bad reputation.

30:7-9

She opens her hands to oppressed people
and stretches them out to needy people.

31:20

FRIENDS AND ENEMIES

No one plans to be an enemy. We all want to be friendly and be a good friend. Yet sometimes things happen that tear down our relationships rather than building them up. Let the wise thoughts that follow help you develop friendships and cope with enemies.

Do not hold back anything good
  from those who are entitled to it
    when you have the power to do so.
When you have the good thing with you,
    do not tell your neighbor,
  "Go away!
  Come back tomorrow.
  I'll give you something then."

Do not plan to do something wrong to your neighbor
  while he is sitting there with you and suspecting nothing.

3:27-29

Whoever walks with wise people will be wise,
  but whoever associates with fools will suffer.

13:20

Whoever forgives an offense seeks love,
  but whoever keeps bringing up the issue
    separates the closest of friends. . . .
A friend always loves,
  and a brother is born to share trouble.

17:9,17

A loner is out to get what he wants for himself.
He opposes all sound reasoning.

18:1

Flipping a coin ends quarrels
  and settles ⌊issues⌋ between powerful people.
An offended brother is more ⌊resistant⌋ than a strong city,
  and disputes are like the locked gate of a castle tower. . . .
Friends can destroy one another,
  But a loving friend can stick closer than family.

18:18-19,24

Wealth adds many friends,
but a poor person is separated from his friend. . . .
Many try to win the kindness of a generous person,
and everyone is a friend to a person who gives gifts.
The entire family of a poor person hates him.
How much more do his friends
keep their distance from him!
When he chases them with words, they are gone.

19:4,6-7

A person with good sense is patient,
and it is to his credit that he overlooks an offense. . . .
A person who has a hot temper will pay for it.
If you rescue him, you will have to do it over and over. . . .
Loyalty is desirable in a person,
and it is better to be poor than a liar.

19:11,19,22

A motive in the human heart is like deep water,
and a person who has understanding draws it out.
Many people declare themselves loyal,
but who can find someone who is ⌊really⌋ trustworthy? . . .
Do not say, "I'll get even with you!"
Wait for the LORD, and he will save you.

20:5-6,22

The mind of a wicked person desires evil
and has no consideration for his neighbor. . . .
A gift ⌊given⌋ in secret calms anger,
and a secret bribe calms great fury.

21:10,14

Do not eat the food of one who is stingy,
and do not crave his delicacies.
As he calculates the cost to himself, this is what he does:
He tells you, "Eat and drink,"
but he doesn't really mean it.

You will vomit the little bit you have eaten
and spoil your pleasant conversation.

23:6-8

Do not be happy when your enemy falls,
and do not feel glad when he stumbles.
The LORD will see it, he won't like it,
and he will turn his anger away from that person.

24:17-18

Fear the LORD, my son.
Fear the king as well.
Do not associate with those who always insist upon change,
because disaster will come to them suddenly.
Who knows what misery both may bring?

24:21-22

Do not set foot in your neighbor's house too often.
Otherwise, he will see too much of you and hate you.

25:17

⌊Like⌋ a broken tooth and a lame foot,
⌊so⌋ is confidence in an unfaithful person
in a ⌊time of⌋ crisis. . . .
If your enemy is hungry, give him some food to eat,
and if he is thirsty, give him some water to drink.
⌊In this way⌋ you will make him feel guilty and ashamed,
and the LORD will reward you.

25:19,21-22

Like a madman who shoots flaming arrows, arrows, and death,
so is the person who tricks his neighbor
and says, "I was only joking!"

26:18-19

A stone is heavy, and sand weighs a lot,
but annoyance caused by a stubborn fool
is heavier than both. . . .
Perfume and incense make the heart glad,
but the sweetness of a friend is a fragrant forest.
Do not abandon your friend or your father's friend.
Do not go to a relative's home when you are in trouble.
A neighbor living nearby is better than a relative far away.

27:3,9-10

Whoever blesses his friend early in the morning
with a loud voice—
his blessing is considered a curse. . . .
⌊As⌋ iron sharpens iron,
so one person sharpens the wits of another.

27:14,17

Showing partiality is not good,
because some people will turn on you
even for a piece of bread.

28:21

GOD'S ATTRIBUTES

Focusing on God's incredible nature can build our faith and trust in him. In the different circumstances of life, we need to remember that he is sovereign, omnipresent, and omnipotent. These Proverbs have something to say about who God is.

By Wisdom the LORD laid the foundation of the earth.
By understanding he established the heavens.
By his knowledge the deep waters were divided,
and the skies dropped dew.

3:19-20

The LORD already possessed me long ago,
when his way began,
before any of his works.
I was appointed from everlasting
from the first,
before the earth began.
I was born
before there were oceans
before there were springs filled with water.
I was born
before the mountains were settled in their places
and before the hills,
when he had not yet made land or fields
or the first dust of the world.

8:22-26

The eyes of the LORD are everywhere.
They watch evil people and good people. . . .
If Sheol and Abaddon lie open in front of the LORD
how much more the human heart!

15:3,11

The plans of the heart belong to humans,
but an answer on the tongue comes from the LORD.
A person thinks all his ways are pure,
but the LORD weighs motives.

16:1-2

The LORD has made everything for his own purpose,
even wicked people for the day of trouble.

16:4

A person may plan his own journey,
but the LORD directs his steps. . . .
The dice are thrown,
but the LORD determines every outcome.

16:9,33

The crucible is for refining silver and the smelter for gold,
but the one who purifies hearts ⌊by fire⌋ is the LORD.

17:3

Many plans are in the human heart,
but the advice of the LORD will endure.

19:21

The LORD is the one who directs a person's steps.
How then can anyone understand his own way?

20:24

The king's heart is like streams of water.
Both are under the LORD's control.
He turns them in any direction he chooses.

21:1

A person thinks everything he does is right,
but the LORD weighs hearts.

21:2

No wisdom, no understanding, and no advice
⌊can stand up⌋ against the LORD.
The horse is made ready for the day of battle,
but the victory belongs to the LORD.

21:30-31

The LORD's eyes watch over knowledge,
but he overturns the words of a treacherous person.

22:12

Do not move an ancient boundary marker
   or enter fields that belong to orphans,
      because the one who is responsible for them is strong.
         He will plead their case against you.

23:10-11

Do not be happy when your enemy falls,
   and do not feel glad when he stumbles.
      The LORD will see it, he won't like it,
         and he will turn his anger away from that person.

24:17-18

It is the glory of God to hide things
   but the glory of kings to investigate them.

25:2

A poor person and an oppressor have this in common:
   The LORD gives both of them sight.

29:13

Many seek an audience with a ruler,
   but justice for humanity comes from the LORD.

29:26

This man's declaration:
   "I'm weary, O God.
   I'm weary and worn out, O God.
   I'm more ⌊like⌋ a dumb animal than a human being.
   I don't ⌊even⌋ have human understanding.
   I haven't learned wisdom.
   I don't have knowledge of the Holy One.

"Who has gone up to heaven and come down?
Who has gathered the wind in the palm of his hand?
Who has wrapped water in a garment?
Who has set up the earth from one end to the other?
What is his name or the name of his son?
   Certainly, you must know!

"Every word of God has proven to be true.
He is a shield to those who come to him for protection.
Do not add to his words,
or he will reprimand you, and you will be found to be a liar."

30:1-6

GUIDANCE, COUNSELING, AND ADVICE

The Spirit's influence in our lives provides us with a path for gaining wisdom. Sometimes we need additional help to follow the path God has chosen for us. For those times, the Proverbs are filled with instructions about the necessity of seeking godly counsel. How wonderful that God provides support from many sources.

Guidance, Counseling, and Advice

My son,
obey the command of your father,
and do not disregard the teachings of your mother.
Fasten them on your heart forever.
Hang them around your neck.
When you walk around, they will lead you.
When you lie down, they will watch over you.
When you wake up, they will talk to you
because the command is a lamp,
the teachings are a light,
and the warnings from discipline
are the path of life
to keep you from an evil woman
and from the smooth talk
of a loose woman.

6:20-24

A nation will fall when there is no direction,
but with many advisers there is victory. . . .
The desire of righteous people ends only in good,
but the hope of wicked people ends only in fury. . . .
Whoever eagerly seeks good searches for good will,
but whoever looks for evil finds it.

11:14,23,27

The thoughts of righteous people are fair.
The advice of wicked people is treacherous.

12:5

A stubborn fool considers his own way the right one,
but a person who listens to advice is wise. . . .
Deceit is in the heart of those who plan evil,
but joy belongs to those who advise peace. . . .
A righteous person looks out for his neighbor,
but the path of wicked people leads others astray.

12:15,20,26

Arrogance produces only quarreling,
   but those who take advice gain wisdom. . . .
The teachings of a wise person are a fountain of life
   to turn ⌊one⌋ away from the grasp of death.

13:10,14

A mocker searches for wisdom without finding it,
   but knowledge comes easily
      to a person who has understanding. . . .

Stay away from a fool,
   because you will not receive knowledge from his lips. . . .
There is a way that seems right to a person,
   but eventually it ends in death.

14:6-7,12

A mocker does not appreciate a warning.
   He will not go to wise people. . . .
Without advice plans go wrong,
   but with many advisers they succeed.

15:12,22

A person may plan his own journey,
   but the LORD directs his steps. . . .
A wise person's heart controls his speech,
   and what he says helps others learn. . . .
There is a way that seems right to a person,
   but eventually it ends in death. . . .
The dice are thrown,
   but the LORD determines every outcome.

16:9,23,25,33

The mind of a person who has understanding
      acquires knowledge.
The ears of wise people seek knowledge.

18:15

A motive in the human heart is like deep water,
and a person who has understanding draws it out.

20:5

The ear that hears,
the eye that sees—
the LORD made them both.

20:12

Plans are confirmed by getting advice,
and with guidance one wages war.

20:18

It is a trap for a person to say impulsively,
"This is a holy offering!"
and later to have second thoughts about those vows.

20:25

A person thinks everything he does is right,
but the LORD weighs hearts.
Doing what is right and fair
is more acceptable to the LORD than offering a sacrifice.

21:2-3

Open your ears, and hear the words of wise people,
and set your mind on the knowledge I give you.
It is pleasant if you keep them in mind
⌊so that⌋ they will be on the tip of your tongue,
so that your trust may be in the LORD.
Today I have made them known to you, especially to you.
Didn't I write to you previously with advice and knowledge
in order to teach you the words of truth
so that you can give an accurate report
to those who send you?

22:17-21

A strong man knows how to use his strength,
but a person with knowledge is even more powerful.
After all, with the right strategy you can wage war,
and with many advisers there is victory.

24:5-6

⌊Like⌋ grabbing a dog by the ears,
⌊so⌋ is a bystander who gets involved
in someone else's quarrel.

26:17

GULLIBILITY AND SENSIBILITY

One of the characteristics of wisdom is being sensible, seeking God's perspective when facing the perplexities of life. If we consider the Proverbs and all of God's Word as essential to our well being, we will avoid becoming the fool that these wise sayings talk about.

Gullibility and Sensibility

The proverbs of Solomon, David's son who was king of Israel, ⌊given⌋
to grasp wisdom and discipline,
to understand deep thoughts,
to acquire the discipline of wise behavior—
righteousness and justice and fairness—
to give insight to gullible people,
to give knowledge and foresight to the young—
a wise person will listen and continue to learn,
and an understanding person will gain direction—
to understand a proverb and a clever saying,
the words of wise people and their riddles.

1:1-6

Gullible people kill themselves because of their turning away.
Fools destroy themselves because of their indifference.
But whoever listens to me will live without worry
and will be free from the dread of disaster.

1:32-33

From a window in my house I looked through my screen.
I was looking at gullible people
when I saw a young man without much sense
among youths.
He was crossing a street near her corner
and walking toward her house
in the twilight,
in the evening,
in the dark hours of the night.

A woman with an ulterior motive meets him.
She is dressed as a prostitute.
She is loud and rebellious.
Her feet will not stay at home.
One moment she is out on the street,
the next she is at the curb,
on the prowl at every corner.
She grabs him and kisses him and brazenly says to him,

"I have some sacrificial meat.
  Today I kept my vows.
That's why I came to meet you.
  Eagerly, I looked for you,
    and I've found you.
I've made my bed,
  with colored sheets of Egyptian linen.
I've sprinkled my bed with myrrh, aloes, and cinnamon.
Come, let's drink our fill of love until morning.
  Let's enjoy making love,
    because my husband's not home.
      He has gone on a long trip.
      He took lots of money with him.
      He won't be home for a couple of weeks."

With all her seductive charms, she persuades him.
With her smooth lips, she makes him give in.
  He immediately follows her
    like a steer on its way to be slaughtered,
    like a ram hobbling into captivity
      until an arrow pierces his heart,
    like a bird darting into a trap.
  He does not realize that it will cost him his life.

Now, sons,
  listen to me.
  Pay attention to the words from my mouth.
    Do not let your heart be turned to her ways.
    Do not wander onto her paths,
      because she has brought down many victims,
        and she has killed all too many.
      Her home is the way to hell
        and leads to the darkest vaults of death.

7:6-27

Gullibility and Sensibility

Does not wisdom call out?
Does not understanding raise its voice?
⌊Wisdom⌋ takes its stand on high ground,
  by the wayside where the roads meet,
  near the gates to the city.
  At the entrance ⌊wisdom⌋ sings its song,
    "I am calling to all of you,
      and my appeal is to all people.
        You gullible people, learn how to be sensible.
        You fools, get a heart that has understanding."

8:1-5

Wisdom has built her house.
She has carved out her seven pillars.
She has prepared her meat.
She has mixed her wine.
She has set her table.
She has sent out her servant girls.
She calls from the highest places in the city,
  "Whoever is gullible turn in here!"

She says to a person without sense,
  "Come, eat my bread,
    and drink the wine I have mixed.
  Stop being gullible and live.
  Start traveling the road to understanding."

9:1-6

The woman Stupidity is loud, gullible, and ignorant.
She sits at the doorway of her house.
She is enthroned on the high ground of the city
  and calls to those who pass by,
    those minding their own business,
      "Whoever is gullible turn in here!"

She says to a person without sense,
  "Stolen waters are sweet,
    and food eaten in secret is tasty."

But he does not know
  that the souls of the dead are there,
  that her guests are in the depths of hell.

9:13-18

A sensible person ⌊discreetly⌋ hides knowledge,
  but foolish minds preach stupidity.

12:23

Good sense brings favor,
  but the way of treacherous people is always the same.
Any sensible person acts with knowledge,
  but a fool displays stupidity.

13:15-16

The wisdom of a sensible person guides his way of life,
  but the stupidity of fools misleads them. . . .
A gullible person believes anything,
  but a sensible person watches his step. . . .
Gullible people are gifted with stupidity,
  but sensible people are crowned with knowledge.

14:8,15,18

Stupidity is fun to the one without much sense,
  but a person who has understanding forges straight ahead.

15:21

Better to meet a bear robbed of its cubs
  than a fool ⌊carried away⌋ with his stupidity.

17:12

  A person who gains sense loves himself.
  One who guards understanding finds something good. . . .
A person with good sense is patient,
  and it is to his credit that he overlooks an offense. . . .
Strike a mocker, and a gullible person may learn a lesson.
  Warn an understanding person,
    and he will gain more knowledge.

19:8,11,25

Gullibility and Sensibility

When a mocker is punished, a gullible person becomes wise,
and when a wise person is instructed, he gains knowledge.
21:11

Sensible people foresee trouble and hide ⌊from it⌋,
but gullible people go ahead and suffer ⌊the consequence⌋.
22:3

Sensible people foresee trouble and hide.
Gullible people go ahead ⌊and⌋ suffer.
27:12

HONESTY AND INTEGRITY

God's Word tells it like it is: lying will destroy a life and then play havoc in the lives of the ones we love. Wisdom tells the truth and experiences God's favor.

Remove dishonesty from your mouth.
Put deceptive speech far away from your lips.
Let your eyes look straight ahead
 and your sight be focused in front of you.
Carefully walk a straight path,
 and all your ways will be secure.
Do not lean to the right or to the left.
Walk away from evil.

4:24-27

A good-for-nothing scoundrel is a person
  who has a dishonest mouth.
 He winks his eye,
  makes a signal with his foot,
   ⌊and⌋ points with his fingers.
 He devises evil all the time with a twisted mind.
 He spreads conflict.
  That is why disaster will come on him suddenly.
   In a moment he will be crushed beyond recovery.

There are six things that the LORD hates,
 even seven that are disgusting to him:
  arrogant eyes,
  a lying tongue,
  hands that kill innocent people,
  a mind devising wicked plans,
  feet that are quick to do wrong,
  a dishonest witness spitting out lies,
   and a person who spreads conflict among relatives.

6:12-19

Listen! I am speaking about noble things,
 and my lips will say what is right.
My mouth expresses the truth,
 and wickedness is disgusting to my lips.
Everything I say is fair,
 and there is nothing twisted or crooked in it.

All of it is clear to a person who has understanding
and right to those who have acquired knowledge.
8:6-9

Treasures gained dishonestly profit no one,
but righteousness rescues from death. . . .
Whoever lives honestly will live securely,
but whoever lives dishonestly will be found out.
Whoever winks with his eye causes heartache.
The one who talks foolishly will be thrown down headfirst.
10:2,9-10

The mouth of a righteous person is a fountain of life,
but the mouths of wicked people conceal violence. . . .
Whoever conceals hatred has lying lips.
Whoever spreads slander is a fool.
10:11,18

The way of the LORD is a fortress for an innocent person
but a ruin to those who are troublemakers.
10:29

Dishonest scales are disgusting to the LORD,
but accurate weights are pleasing to him. . . .
Integrity guides decent people,
but hypocrisy leads treacherous people to ruin. . . .
Decent people are saved by their righteousness,
but treacherous people are trapped by their own greed.
11:1,3,6

A wicked person earns dishonest wages,
but whoever spreads righteousness earns honest pay. . . .
Devious people are disgusting to the LORD,
but he is delighted with those whose ways are innocent.
11:18,20

Honesty and Integrity

A good person obtains favor from the LORD,
but the LORD condemns everyone who schemes. . . .
The word of truth lasts forever,
but lies last only a moment.
Deceit is in the heart of those who plan evil,
but joy belongs to those who advise peace. . . .
Lips that lie are disgusting to the LORD,
but honest people are his delight.

12:2,19-20,22

A righteous person hates lying,
but a wicked person behaves with shame and disgrace.
Righteousness protects the honest way of life,
but wickedness ruins a sacrifice for sin.

13:5-6

Whoever lives right fears the LORD,
but a person who is devious in his ways despises him. . . .
The wisdom of a sensible person guides his way of life,
but the stupidity of fools misleads them. . . .
An honest witness saves lives,
but one who tells lies is dangerous.

14:2,8,25

A trustworthy witness does not lie,
but a dishonest witness breathes lies.

14:5

A soothing tongue is a tree of life,
but a deceitful tongue breaks the spirit.

15:4

Better a few ⌊possessions⌋ gained honestly
than many gained through injustice. . . .
Honest balances and scales belong to the LORD.
He made the entire set of weights.

16:8,11

Kings are happy with honest words,
  and whoever speaks what is right is loved. . . .
Whoever winks his eye is plotting something devious.
Whoever bites his lips has finished his evil work.

16:13,30

An evildoer pays attention to wicked lips.
A liar opens his ears to a slanderous tongue. . . .
Refined speech is not fitting for a godless fool.
  How much less does lying fit a noble person!

17:4,7

A bribe seems ⌊like⌋ a jewel to the one who gives it.
  Wherever he turns, he prospers. . . .
  A twisted mind never finds happiness,
    and one with a devious tongue
      ⌊repeatedly⌋ gets into trouble.

17:8,20

Better to be a poor person who lives innocently
  than to be one who talks dishonestly and is a fool. . . .
Loyalty is desirable in a person,
  and it is better to be poor than a liar.

19:1,22

Many people declare themselves loyal,
  but who can find someone who is ⌊really⌋ trustworthy?
A righteous person lives on the basis of his integrity.
  Blessed are his children after he is gone. . . .
A double standard of weights and measures—
  both are disgusting to the LORD.

20:6-7,10

"Bad! Bad!" says the buyer.
  Then, as he goes away, he brags ⌊about his bargain⌋. . . .
Food gained dishonestly tastes sweet to a person,
  but afterwards his mouth will be filled with gravel. . . .

Honesty and Integrity

A double standard of weights is disgusting to the LORD,
  and dishonest scales are no good.

20:14,17,23

Doing what is right and fair
  is more acceptable to the LORD than offering a sacrifice. . . .
Those who gather wealth by lying are wasting time.
  They are looking for death.

21:3,6

The way of a guilty person is crooked,
  but the behavior of those who are pure is moral.

21:8

A lying witness will die,
  but a person who listens to advice will continue to speak.

21:28

A devious person has thorns and traps ahead of him.
  Whoever guards himself will stay far away from them. . . .
Do not move an ancient boundary marker
  that your ancestors set in place.

22:5,28

Whoever plans to do evil will be known as a schemer.
Foolish scheming is sinful,
  and a mocker is disgusting to everyone.

24:8-9

⌊Like⌋ a dense fog or a dust storm,
  ⌊so⌋ is a person who brags about a gift
    that he does not give. . . .

25:14

Whoever is filled with hate disguises it with his speech,
  but inside he holds on to deceit.
    When he talks charmingly, do not trust him
      because of the seven disgusting things in his heart.

His hatred is deceitfully hidden,
but his wickedness will be revealed to the community.
26:24-26

A lying tongue hates its victims,
and a flattering mouth causes ruin.
26:28

Better to be a poor person who has integrity
than to be rich and double-dealing. . . .
Whoever becomes wealthy through ⌊unfair⌋ loans and interest
collects them for the one who is kind to the poor.
28:6,8

Whoever leads decent people into evil will fall into his own pit,
but innocent people will inherit good things. . . .
Whoever covers over his sins does not prosper.
Whoever confesses and abandons them
receives compassion. . . .
Whoever lives honestly will be safe.
Whoever lives dishonestly will fall all at once.
28:10,13,18

Every word of God has proven to be true.
He is a shield to those who come to him for protection.
Do not add to his words,
or he will reprimand you, and you will be found to be a liar.
30:5-6

I've asked you for two things.
Don't keep them from me before I die:
Keep vanity and lies far away from me.
Don't give me either poverty or riches.
Feed me ⌊only⌋ the food I need,
or I may feel satisfied and deny you
and say, 'Who is the LORD?'
or I may become poor and steal
and give the name of my God a bad reputation.
30:7-9

JEALOUSY AND ENVY

When we feel insecure, we can easily become jealous or envious. God lets us know that these feelings will not bring the good results we desire in relationships. Avoiding these destructive feelings helps us to lead healthy, happy lives.

Jealousy and Envy

Whoever commits adultery with a woman has no sense.
Whoever does this destroys himself.
An adulterous man will find disease and dishonor,
and his disgrace will not be blotted out,
because jealousy arouses a husband's fury.
The husband will show no mercy
when he takes revenge.
No amount of money will change his mind.
The largest bribe will not satisfy him.

6:32-35

A tranquil heart makes for a healthy body,
but jealousy is ⌊like⌋ bone cancer.

14:30

Do not envy sinners in your heart.
Instead, continue to fear the LORD.
There is indeed a future,
and your hope will never be cut off.

23:17-18

Do not envy evil people
or wish you were with them,
because their minds plot violence,
and their lips talk trouble. . . .
Do not get overly upset with evildoers.
Do not envy wicked people,
because an evil person has no future,
and the lamps of wicked people will be snuffed out.

24:1-2,19-20

Anger is cruel, and fury is overwhelming,
but who can survive jealousy?

27:4

JOY AND SADNESS

Happiness is something that happens to you, but joy is something you choose. Joy comes from right choices and trusting in God's ability to bring good out of disaster. God's Word shares many insights for choosing joy.

Wisdom sings her song in the streets.
    In the public squares she raises her voice.
    At the corners of noisy streets she calls out.
    At the entrances to the city she speaks her words,
        "How long will you gullible people
            love being so gullible?
        How long will you mockers find joy in your mocking?
        How long will you fools hate knowledge?"

1:20-22

⌊Wisdom will⌋ save you
    from the way of evil,
    from the person who speaks devious things,
    from those who abandon the paths of righteousness
        to walk the ways of darkness,
    from those who enjoy doing evil,
    from those who find joy in the deviousness of evil.
        Their paths are crooked.
        Their ways are devious.

2:12-15

When he set up the heavens, I was there.
When he traced the horizon on the surface of the ocean,
when he established the skies above,
when he determined the currents in the ocean,
when he set a limit for the sea
    so the waters would not overstep his command,
when he traced the foundations of the earth,
    I was beside him as a master craftsman.
    I made him happy day after day,
        I rejoiced in front of him all the time,
            found joy in his inhabited world,
                and delighted in the human race.

8:27-31

Like the laughter of a fool when he carries out an evil plan,
so is wisdom to a person who has understanding.

10:23

The hope of righteous people ⌊leads to⌋ joy,
but the eager waiting of wicked people comes to nothing.

10:28

When righteous people prosper, a city is glad.
When wicked people die, there are songs of joy.

11:10

Deceit is in the heart of those who plan evil,
but joy belongs to those who advise peace.

12:20

A person's anxiety will weigh him down,
but an encouraging word makes him joyful.

12:25

A fulfilled desire is sweet to the soul,
but turning from evil is disgusting to fools.

13:19

The heart knows its own bitterness,
and no stranger can share its joy. . . .
Even while laughing a heart can ache,
and joy can end in grief.

14:10,13

A joyful heart makes a cheerful face,
but with a heartache comes depression.

15:13

Every day is a terrible day for a miserable person,
but a cheerful heart has a continual feast.

15:15

Joy and Sadness

Stupidity is fun to the one without much sense,
  but a person who has understanding forges straight ahead.

15:21

A person is delighted to hear an answer from his own mouth,
  and a timely word—oh, how good! . . .
A twinkle in the eye delights the heart.
  Good news refreshes the body.

15:23,30

  A twisted mind never finds happiness,
    and one with a devious tongue
      ⌊repeatedly⌋ gets into trouble. . . .
A joyful heart is good medicine,
  but depression drains one's strength.

17:20,22

The parent of a fool has grief,
  and the father of a godless fool has no joy. . . .
A foolish son is a heartache to his father
  and bitter grief to his mother.

17:21,25

A fool does not find joy in understanding
  but only in expressing his own opinion.

18:2

A person's spirit can endure sickness,
  but who can bear a broken spirit?

18:14

My son,
  if you have a wise heart,
    my heart will rejoice as well.
    My heart rejoices when you speak what is right. . . .
  A righteous person's father will certainly rejoice.
  Someone who has a wise son will enjoy him.

May your father and your mother be glad.
May she who gave birth to you rejoice.

23:15-16,24-25

Do not be happy when your enemy falls,
and do not feel glad when he stumbles.
The LORD will see it, he won't like it,
and he will turn his anger away from that person.

24:17-18

These also are the sayings of wise people:

Showing partiality as a judge is not good.
Whoever says to a guilty person, "You are innocent,"
will be cursed by people and condemned by nations.
But people will be pleased with those
who convict a guilty person,
and a great blessing will come to them.

24:23-25

When you find honey, eat only as much as you need.
Otherwise, you will have too much and vomit.

25:16

⌊Like⌋ cold water to a thirsty soul,
so is good news from far away.

25:25

Perfume and incense make the heart glad,
but the sweetness of a friend is a fragrant forest.

27:9

Be wise, my son, and make my heart glad
so that I can answer anyone who criticizes me.

27:11

Blessed is the one who is always fearful ⌊of sin⌋,
but whoever is hard-hearted falls into disaster.

28:14

To an evil person sin is bait in a trap,
but a righteous person runs away from it and is glad.

29:6

Without prophetic vision people run wild,
but blessed are those who follow ⌊God's⌋ teachings.

29:18

The bloodsucking leech has two daughters—"Give!" and "Give!"
Three things are never satisfied.
Four never say, "Enough!":
the grave,
a barren womb,
a land that never gets enough water,
a fire that does not say, "Enough!"

30:15-16

She seeks out wool and linen ⌊with care⌋
and works with willing hands. . . .
She dresses with strength and nobility,
and she smiles at the future.

31:13,25

JUSTICE AND IMPARTIALITY

Although we don't always see justice fulfilled on this earth, we know that God is a fair God. He promises to deliver appropriate consequences on those who deserve it. That's why these Proverbs admonish us not to take justice into our own hands.

Justice and Impartiality

The proverbs of Solomon, David's son who was king of Israel, ⌊given⌋
to grasp wisdom and discipline,
to understand deep thoughts,
to acquire the discipline of wise behavior—
righteousness and justice and fairness—
to give insight to gullible people,
to give knowledge and foresight to the young—
a wise person will listen and continue to learn,
and an understanding person will gain direction—
to understand a proverb and a clever saying,
the words of wise people and their riddles.

1:1-6

The LORD gives wisdom.
From his mouth come knowledge and understanding.
He has reserved priceless wisdom for decent people.
He is a shield for those who walk in integrity
in order to guard those on paths of justice
and to watch over the way of his godly ones.
Then you will understand what is right and just and fair—
every good course ⌊in life⌋.

2:6-9

I, Understanding, have strength.
Through me kings reign,
and rulers decree fair laws.
Through me princes rule,
so do nobles and all fair judges.
I love those who love me.
Those eagerly looking for me will find me.
I have riches and honor,
lasting wealth and righteousness.
What I produce is better than gold, pure gold.
What I yield is better than fine silver.
I walk in the way of righteousness, on the paths of justice,
to give an inheritance to those who love me
and to fill their treasuries.

8:14b-21

A righteous person is rescued from trouble,
  and a wicked person takes his place. . . .
As righteousness leads to life,
  so whoever pursues evil finds his own death. . . .
Certainly, an evil person will not go unpunished,
  but the descendants of righteous people will escape.

11:8,19,21

The fruit of a righteous person is a tree of life,
  and a winner of souls is wise.
If the righteous person is rewarded on earth,
  how much more the wicked person and the sinner!

11:30-31

Overthrow wicked people, and they are no more,
  but the families of righteous people continue to stand.

12:7

Everlasting life is on the way of righteousness.
Eternal death is not along its path.

12:28

The light of righteous people beams brightly,
  but the lamp of wicked people will be snuffed out.

13:9

Wealth ⌊gained⌋ through injustice dwindles away,
  but whoever gathers little by little has plenty. . . .
When poor people are able to plow, there is much food,
  but a person is swept away where there is no justice.

13:11,23

Evil people will bow to good people.
Wicked people will bow at the gates of a righteous person.

14:19

A wicked person is thrown down by his own wrongdoing,
but even in his death a righteous person has a refuge.
Wisdom finds rest in the heart of an understanding person.
Even fools recognize this.

14:32-33

Whoever is greedy for unjust gain brings trouble to his family,
but whoever hates bribes will live.

15:27

Honest balances and scales belong to the LORD.
He made the entire set of weights.

16:11

A rebel looks for nothing but evil.
Therefore, a cruel messenger will be sent
⌊to punish⌋ him. . . .
Whoever pays back evil for good—
evil will never leave his home.

17:11,13

A wicked person secretly accepts a bribe
to corrupt the ways of justice.

17:23

To punish an innocent person is not good.
To strike down noble people is not right.

17:26

It is not good to be partial toward a wicked person,
thereby depriving an innocent person of justice.

18:5

The first to state his case seems right
⌊until⌋ his neighbor comes to cross-examine him.

18:17

A lying witness will not go unpunished.
One who tells lies will not escape. . . .
A lying witness will not go unpunished.
One who tells lies will die.

19:5,9

Whoever obeys the law preserves his life,
⌊but⌋ whoever despises the LORD's ways will be put to death.

19:16

A worthless witness mocks justice,
and the mouths of wicked people swallow up trouble.
Punishments are set for mockers
and beatings for the backs of fools.

19:28-29

A king who sits on his throne to judge
sifts out every evil with his eyes.

20:8

A double standard of weights and measures—
both are disgusting to the LORD. . . .
A double standard of weights is disgusting to the LORD,
and dishonest scales are no good.

20:10,23

Do not say, "I'll get even with you!"
Wait for the LORD, and he will save you.

20:22

Doing what is right and fair
is more acceptable to the LORD than offering a sacrifice. . . .
The violence of wicked people will drag them away
since they refuse to do what is just. . . .
A righteous person wisely considers the house
of a wicked person.
He throws wicked people into disasters.

21:3,7,12

Whoever shuts his ear to the cry of the poor
will call and not be answered.

21:13

A gift ⌊given⌋ in secret calms anger,
and a secret bribe calms great fury.
When justice is done, a righteous person is delighted,
but troublemakers are terrified. . . .
Wicked people become a ransom for righteous people,
and treacherous people will take the place
of decent people.

21:14-15,18

Whoever plants injustice will harvest trouble,
and this weapon of his own fury will be destroyed. . . .
Do not rob the poor because they are poor
or trample on the rights of an oppressed person
at the city gate,
because the LORD will plead their case
and will take the lives of those who rob them.

22:8,22-23

Do not move an ancient boundary marker
that your ancestors set in place. . . .
Do not move an ancient boundary marker
or enter fields that belong to orphans,
because the one who is responsible for them is strong.
He will plead their case against you.

22:28;23:10-11

Rescue captives condemned to death,
and spare those staggering toward their slaughter.
When you say, "We didn't know this,"
won't the one who weighs hearts take note of it?
Won't the one who guards your soul know it?
Won't he pay back people for what they do?

24:11-12

You wicked one,
do not lie in ambush at the home of a righteous person.
Do not rob his house.
A righteous person may fall seven times,
but he gets up again.
However, in a disaster wicked people fall.

24:15-16

Do not be happy when your enemy falls,
and do not feel glad when he stumbles.
The LORD will see it, he won't like it,
and he will turn his anger away from that person.

24:17-18

These also are the sayings of wise people:

Showing partiality as a judge is not good.
Whoever says to a guilty person, "You are innocent,"
will be cursed by people and condemned by nations.
But people will be pleased with those
who convict a guilty person,
and a great blessing will come to them.

24:23-25

Do not testify against your neighbor without a reason,
and do not deceive with your lips.
Do not say,
"I'll treat him as he treated me.
I'll pay him back for what he has done to me."

24:28-29

Do not be in a hurry to go to court.
What will you do in the end if your neighbor disgraces you?
Present your argument to your neighbor,
but do not reveal another person's secret.
Otherwise, when he hears about it,
he will humiliate you,
and his evil report about you will never disappear.

25:8-10

Justice and Impartiality

If your enemy is hungry, give him some food to eat,
and if he is thirsty, give him some water to drink.
⌊In this way⌋ you will make him feel guilty and ashamed,
and the LORD will reward you.

25:21-22

Whoever digs a pit will fall into it.
Whoever rolls a stone will have it roll back on him.

26:27

Evil people do not understand justice,
but those who seek the LORD understand everything.

28:5

Whoever leads decent people into evil will fall into his own pit,
but innocent people will inherit good things.

28:10

A leader without understanding taxes ⌊his people⌋ heavily,
but those who hate unjust gain will live longer.

28:16

A person burdened with the guilt of murder
will be a fugitive down to his grave.
No one will help him.

28:17

Showing partiality is not good,
because some people will turn on you
even for a piece of bread.

28:21

By means of justice, a king builds up a country,
but a person who confiscates religious contributions
tears it down. . . .
A righteous person knows the just cause of the poor.
A wicked person does not understand this.

29:4,7

When a wise person goes to court with a stubborn fool,
he may rant and rave,
but there is no peace and quiet.
Bloodthirsty people hate an innocent person,
but decent people seek ⌊to protect⌋ his life.
A fool expresses all his emotions,
but a wise person controls them.

29:9-11

A poor person and an oppressor have this in common:
The LORD gives both of them sight.
When a king judges the poor with honesty,
his throne will always be secure. . . .
When wicked people increase, crime increases,
but righteous people will witness their downfall.

29:13-14,16

Many seek an audience with a ruler,
but justice for humanity comes from the LORD.

29:26

An unjust person is disgusting to righteous people.
A decent person is disgusting to wicked people.

29:27

Speak out for the one who cannot speak,
for the rights of those who are doomed.
Speak out,
judge fairly,
and defend the rights of oppressed and needy people.

31:8-9

KINDNESS

Our ability to be kind is based in remembering that God hasn't dealt us the punishment that we deserve. We can share the kindness God has shown us with others we meet. Being gentle and understanding, even compassionate, will bring us the results we want in life.

Kindness

A gracious woman wins respect,
  but ruthless men gain riches.

11:16

A merciful person helps himself,
  but a cruel person hurts himself.

11:17

A righteous person cares ⌊even⌋ about the life of his animals,
  but the compassion of wicked people is ⌊nothing but⌋ cruelty.

12:10

Whoever despises his neighbor sins,
  but blessed is the one who is kind to humble people.

14:21

Don't those who stray plan what is evil,
  while those who are merciful and faithful plan what is good?

14:22

Whoever oppresses the poor insults his maker,
  but whoever is kind to the needy honors him.

14:31

A gentle answer turns away rage,
  but a harsh word stirs up anger.

15:1

The person who is truly wise is called understanding,
  and speaking sweetly helps others learn.
Understanding is a fountain of life to the one who has it,
  but stubborn fools punish themselves with their stupidity.
A wise person's heart controls his speech,
  and what he says helps others learn.
Pleasant words are ⌊like⌋ honey from a honeycomb—
  sweet to the spirit and healthy for the body.

16:21-24

Whoever makes fun of a poor person insults his maker.
Whoever is happy ⌊to see someone's⌋ distress
will not escape punishment.

17:5

Whoever forgives an offense seeks love,
but whoever keeps bringing up the issue
separates the closest of friends.

17:9

A poor person is timid when begging,
but a rich person is blunt when replying.

18:23

Many try to win the kindness of a generous person,
and everyone is a friend to a person who gives gifts.

19:6

Whoever loves a pure heart and whoever speaks graciously
has a king as his friend.

22:11

If your enemy is hungry, give him some food to eat,
and if he is thirsty, give him some water to drink.
⌊In this way⌋ you will make him feel guilty and ashamed,
and the LORD will reward you.

25:21-22

Whoever becomes wealthy through ⌊unfair⌋ loans and interest
collects them for the one who is kind to the poor.

28:8

She speaks with wisdom,
and on her tongue there is tender instruction.

31:26

LAZINESS AND DILIGENCE

God's Word has some great descriptions of how we appear when we're lazy. It may feel good to us, but it's not a pretty sight! How much better to do the Father's business with enthusiasm. These Proverbs tell us how.

Laziness and Diligence

Consider the ant, you lazy bum.
Watch its ways, and become wise.
Although it has no overseer, officer, or ruler,
in summertime it stores its food supply.
At harvest time it gathers its food.

How long will you lie there, you lazy bum?
When will you get up from your sleep?
"Just a little sleep,
just a little slumber,
just a little nap."
Then your poverty will come ⌊to you⌋ like a drifter,
and your need will come ⌊to you⌋ like a bandit.

6:6-11

Lazy hands bring poverty,
but hard-working hands bring riches.
Whoever gathers in the summer is a wise son.
Whoever sleeps at harvest time brings shame.

10:4-5

Like vinegar to the teeth,
like smoke to the eyes,
so is the lazy person to those who send him ⌊on a mission⌋.

10:26

Hard-working hands gain control,
but lazy hands do slave labor. . . .
A lazy hunter does not catch his prey,
but a hard-working person becomes wealthy.

12:24,27

A lazy person craves food and there is none,
but the appetite of hard-working people is satisfied.

13:4

An undependable messenger gets into trouble,
but a dependable envoy brings healing.

13:17

Where there are no cattle, the feeding trough is empty,
but the strength of an ox produces plentiful harvests.

14:4

The path of lazy people is like a thorny hedge,
but the road of decent people is an ⌊open⌋ highway.

15:19

A laborer's appetite works to his advantage,
because his hunger drives him on.

16:26

Whoever is lazy in his work is related to a vandal.

18:9

Laziness throws one into a deep sleep,
and an idle person will go hungry. . . .
A lazy person puts his fork in his food.
He doesn't even bring it back to his mouth.

19:15,24

A lazy person does not plow in the fall.
He looks for something in the harvest but finds nothing. . . .
Do not love sleep or you will end up poor.
Keep your eyes open, and you will have plenty to eat.

20:4,13

The plans of a hard-working person lead to prosperity,
but everyone who is ⌊always⌋ in a hurry ends up in poverty.

21:5

The desire of a lazy person will kill him
because his hands refuse to work.
All day long he feels greedy,
but a righteous person gives and does not hold back.
21:25-26

A lazy person says,
"There's a lion outside!
I'll be murdered in the streets!"
22:13

Do you see a person who is efficient in his work?
He will serve kings.
He will not serve unknown people.
22:29

Do not wear yourself out getting rich.
Be smart enough to stop.
Will you catch only a fleeting glimpse of wealth
before it is gone?
It makes wings for itself like an eagle flying into the sky.
23:4-5

Live a more disciplined life,
and listen carefully to words of knowledge.
23:12

My son,
listen, be wise,
and keep your mind going in the right direction.
Do not associate with those who drink too much wine,
with those who eat too much meat,
because both a drunk and a glutton will become poor.
Drowsiness will dress a person in rags.
23:19-21

I passed by a lazy person's field,
the vineyard belonging to a person without sense.
I saw that it was all overgrown with thistles.
The ground was covered with weeds,
and its stone fence was torn down.
When I observed ⌞this⌟, I took it to heart.
I saw it and learned my lesson.
"Just a little sleep,
just a little slumber,
just a little nap."
Then your poverty will come like a drifter,
and your need will come like a bandit.

24:30-34

Like the coolness of snow on a harvest day,
⌞so⌟ is a trustworthy messenger to those who send him:
He refreshes his masters.

25:13

⌞Like⌟ a broken tooth and a lame foot,
⌞so⌟ is confidence in an unfaithful person in a ⌞time of⌟ crisis.

25:19

A lazy person says,
"There's a ferocious lion out on the road!
There's a lion loose in the streets!"
⌞As⌟ a door turns on its hinges,
so the lazy person turns on his bed.
A lazy person puts his fork in his food.
He wears himself out as he brings it back to his mouth.
A lazy person thinks he is wiser than seven people
who give a sensible answer.

26:13-16

Be fully aware of the condition of your flock,
and pay close attention to your herds.
Wealth is not forever.
Nor does a crown last from one generation to the next.

⌊When⌋ grass is cut short, the tender growth appears,
and vegetables are gathered on the hills.
Lambs ⌊will provide⌋ you with clothing,
and the money from the male goats will buy a field.
There will be enough goat milk to feed you,
to feed your family,
and to keep your servant girls alive.

27:23-27

Whoever works his land will have plenty to eat.
Whoever chases unrealistic dreams will have plenty of nothing.

28:19

Who can find a wife with a strong character?
She is worth far more than jewels.
Her husband trusts her with ⌊all⌋ his heart,
and he does not lack anything good.
She helps him and never harms him all the days of her life.

She seeks out wool and linen ⌊with care⌋
and works with willing hands.
She is like merchant ships.
She brings her food from far away.
She wakes up while it is still dark
and gives food to her family
and portions of food to her female slaves.

She picks out a field and buys it.
She plants a vineyard from the profits she has earned.
She puts on strength like a belt
and goes to work with energy.
She sees that she is making a good profit.
Her lamp burns late at night.

She puts her hands on the distaff,
  and her fingers hold a spindle.
She opens her hands to oppressed people
  and stretches them out to needy people.
She does not fear for her family when it snows
  because her whole family
    has a double layer of clothing.
She makes quilts for herself.
Her clothes are ⌊made of⌋ linen and purple cloth.

Her husband is known at the city gates
  when he sits with the leaders of the land.

She makes linen garments and sells them
  and delivers belts to the merchants.
She dresses with strength and nobility,
  and she smiles at the future.

She speaks with wisdom,
  and on her tongue there is tender instruction.
She keeps a close eye on the conduct of her family,
  and she does not eat the bread of idleness.
Her children and her husband
  stand up and bless her.
In addition, he sings her praises, by saying,
  'Many women have done noble work,
    but you have surpassed them all!'

Charm is deceptive, and beauty evaporates,
  ⌊but⌋ a woman who has the fear of the LORD
      should be praised.
Reward her for what she has done,
  and let her achievements praise her at the city gates.

31:10-31

LOVE AND HATRED

Love may not make the world go around, but it is God's ultimate expression of His work in our lives. Evangelist Winkie Pratney defines love as "the choice for a person's highest good." God's Word tells us how to make that decision to love.

Love and Hatred

Wisdom sings her song in the streets.
In the public squares she raises her voice.
At the corners of noisy streets she calls out.
At the entrances to the city she speaks her words,
"How long will you gullible people love being so gullible?
How long will you mockers find joy in your mocking?
How long will you fools hate knowledge?

"Turn to me when I warn you.
I will generously pour out my spirit for you.
I will make my words known to you.

"I called, and you refused to listen.
I stretched out my hands to you,
and no one paid attention.
You ignored all my advice.
You did not want me to warn you.
I will laugh at your calamity.
I will make fun of you
when panic strikes you,
when panic strikes you like a violent storm,
when calamity strikes you like a wind storm,
when trouble and anguish come to you.

"They will call to me at that time, but I will not answer.
They will look for me, but they will not find me,
because they hated knowledge
and did not choose the fear of the LORD.
They refused my advice.
They despised my every warning.
They will eat the fruit of their lifestyle.
They will be stuffed with their own schemes.

"Gullible people kill themselves
because of their turning away.
Fools destroy themselves because of their indifference.
But whoever listens to me will live without worry
and will be free from the dread of disaster."

1:20-33

Do not reject the discipline of the LORD, my son,
  and do not resent his warning,
    because the LORD warns the one he loves,
      even as a father warns a son with whom he is pleased.

3:11-12

Do not abandon wisdom, and it will watch over you.
Love wisdom, and it will protect you.

4:6

Drink water out of your own cistern
  and running water from your own well.
    Why should water flow out of your spring?
    Why should your streams flow into the streets?
      They should be yours alone,
        so do not share them with strangers.
Let your own fountain be blessed,
  and enjoy the girl you married when you were young,
    a loving doe and a graceful deer.
  Always let her breasts satisfy you.
  Always be intoxicated with her love.
    Why should you, my son,
      be intoxicated with an adulterous woman
        and fondle a loose woman's breast?

5:15-20

I, Wisdom, live with insight,
  and I acquire knowledge and foresight.
    To fear the LORD is to hate evil.
  I hate pride, arrogance, evil behavior, and twisted speech.
    Advice and priceless wisdom are mine.
I, Understanding, have strength.
  Through me kings reign,
    and rulers decree fair laws.
  Through me princes rule,
    so do nobles and all fair judges.
I love those who love me.
  Those eagerly looking for me will find me.

I have riches and honor,
  lasting wealth and righteousness.
What I produce is better than gold, pure gold.
What I yield is better than fine silver.
I walk in the way of righteousness, on the paths of justice,
  to give an inheritance to those who love me
    and to fill their treasuries.

8:12-21

Whoever corrects a mocker receives abuse.
Whoever warns a wicked person gets hurt.
  Do not warn a mocker, or he will hate you.
  Warn a wise person, and he will love you.
    Give ⌊advice⌋ to a wise person,
      and he will become even wiser.
    Teach a righteous person,
      and he will learn more.

9:7-9

Hate starts quarrels,
  but love covers every wrong.

10:12

Whoever guarantees a stranger's loan will get into trouble,
  but whoever hates the closing of a deal remains secure.

11:15

Whoever loves discipline loves to learn,
  but whoever hates correction is a dumb animal.

12:1

A person will be praised based on his insight,
  but whoever has a twisted mind will be despised.

12:8

A righteous person hates lying,
  but a wicked person behaves with shame and disgrace.

13:5

Whoever refuses to spank his son hates him,
  but whoever loves his son disciplines him from early on.
13:24

A short-tempered person acts stupidly,
  and a person who plots evil is hated.
14:17

A poor person is hated even by his neighbor,
  but a rich person is loved by many.
Whoever despises his neighbor sins,
  but blessed is the one who is kind to humble people.
14:20-21

The way of wicked people is disgusting to the LORD,
  but he loves those who pursue righteousness.
Discipline is a terrible ⌊burden⌋ to anyone
    who leaves the ⌊right⌋ path.
  Anyone who hates a warning will die.
15:9-10

Better to have a dish of vegetables where there is love
  than juicy steaks where there is hate.
15:17

A wise son makes his father happy,
  but a foolish child despises its mother. . . .
Whoever is greedy for unjust gain brings trouble to his family,
  but whoever hates bribes will live. . . .
Whoever ignores discipline despises himself,
  but the person who listens to warning gains understanding.
15:20,27,32

Kings are happy with honest words,
  and whoever speaks what is right is loved.
16:13

Love and Hatred

Whoever forgives an offense seeks love,
but whoever keeps bringing up the issue
separates the closest of friends. . . .
A friend always loves,
and a brother is born to share trouble.

17:9,17

Whoever loves sin loves a quarrel.
Whoever builds his city gate high invites destruction.

17:19

The tongue has the power of life and death,
and those who love to talk will have to eat their own words.

18:21

A person who gains sense loves himself.
One who guards understanding finds something good.

19:8

Many people declare themselves loyal,
but who can find someone who is ⌊really⌋ trustworthy?

20:6

Do not love sleep or you will end up poor.
Keep your eyes open, and you will have plenty to eat.

20:13

Whoever loves pleasure will become poor.
Whoever loves wine and expensive food will not become rich.

21:17

Whoever loves a pure heart and whoever speaks graciously
has a king as his friend.

22:11

When you sit down to eat with a ruler,
pay close attention to what is in front of you,
and put a knife to your throat if you have a big appetite.

Do not crave his delicacies,
because this is food that deceives you. . . .
Do not eat the food of one who is stingy,
and do not crave his delicacies.
As he calculates the cost to himself, this is what he does:
He tells you, "Eat and drink,"
but he doesn't really mean it.
You will vomit the little bit you have eaten
and spoil your pleasant conversation.

23:1-3,6-8

Do not set foot in your neighbor's house too often.
Otherwise, he will see too much of you and hate you.

25:17

Whoever is filled with hate disguises it with his speech,
but inside he holds on to deceit.
When he talks charmingly, do not trust him
because of the seven disgusting things in his heart.
His hatred is deceitfully hidden,
but his wickedness will be revealed to the community.

26:24-26

A lying tongue hates its victims,
and a flattering mouth causes ruin.

26:28

Open criticism is better than unexpressed love.

27:5

One who is full despises honey,
but to one who is hungry,
even bitter food tastes sweet.

27:7

A leader without understanding taxes ⌊his people⌋ heavily,
but those who hate unjust gain will live longer.

28:16

A person who loves wisdom makes his father happy,
but one who pays prostitutes wastes his wealth.

29:3

Bloodthirsty people hate an innocent person,
but decent people seek ⌊to protect⌋ his life.

29:10

Whoever is a thief's partner hates his own life.
He will not testify under oath.

29:24

The eye that makes fun of a father
and hates to obey a mother
will be plucked out by ravens in the valley
and eaten by young vultures.

30:17

Three things cause the earth to tremble,
even four it cannot bear up under:
a slave when he becomes king,
a godless fool when he is filled with food,
a woman who is unloved when she gets married,
a maid when she replaces her mistress.

30:21-23

MALICIOUS TALK

Talking about others is a habit we need to avoid. God's Word clearly warns us about this damaging and painful temptation. Let's pay close attention.

Malicious Talk

Whoever gossips gives away secrets,
but whoever is trustworthy in spirit can keep a secret.
11:13

A devious person spreads quarrels.
A gossip separates the closest of friends.
16:28

Whoever forgives an offense seeks love,
but whoever keeps bringing up the issue
separates the closest of friends.
17:9

The words of a gossip are swallowed greedily,
and they go down into a person's innermost being.
18:8

Whoever goes around as a gossip tells secrets.
Do not associate with a person whose mouth is always open.
20:19

Present your argument to your neighbor,
but do not reveal another person's secret.
Otherwise, when he hears about it, he will humiliate you,
and his evil report about you will never disappear.
25:9-10

Without wood a fire goes out,
and without gossip a quarrel dies down. . . .
The words of a gossip are swallowed greedily,
and they go down into a person's innermost being.
26:20,22

MARRIAGE

It's amazing how we look forward to getting married, but afterward wonder why we were so enthused about this challenging step in life. The wisdom of the Proverbs enlightens us on how to fulfill God's plan for oneness and unity.

Marriage

⌊Like⌋ a gold ring in a pig's snout,
⌊so⌋ is a beautiful woman who lacks good taste.

11:22

Whoever brings trouble upon his family inherits ⌊only⌋ wind,
and that stubborn fool becomes a slave to the wise in heart.

11:29

A wife with strength of character is the crown of her husband,
but the wife who disgraces him is like bone cancer.

12:4

The wisest of women builds up her home,
but a stupid one tears it down with her own hands.

14:1

Better to have a little with the fear of the LORD
than great treasure and turmoil.
Better to have a dish of vegetables where there is love
than juicy steaks where there is hate.

15:16-17

Whoever finds a wife finds something good
and has obtained favor from the LORD.

18:22

A foolish son ruins his father,
and a quarreling woman is like constantly dripping water.
Home and wealth are inherited from fathers,
but a sensible wife comes from the LORD.

19:13-14

Better to live on a corner of a roof
than to share a home with a quarreling woman.

21:9

Better to live in a desert
  than with a quarreling and angry woman.

21:19

The mouth of an adulterous woman is a deep pit.
  The one who is cursed by the LORD will fall into it.

22:14

My son,
  give me your heart.
  Let your eyes find happiness in my ways.
    A prostitute is a deep pit.
    A loose woman is a narrow well.
    She is like a robber, lying in ambush.
    She spreads unfaithfulness throughout society.

23:26-28

Better to live on a corner of a roof
  than to share a home with a quarreling woman.

25:24

Like a bird wandering from its nest,
  so is a husband wandering from his home.

27:8

Constantly dripping water on a rainy day
    is like a quarreling woman.
  Whoever can control her can control the wind.
    He can even pick up olive oil with his right hand.

27:15-16

Three things are never satisfied.
Four never say, "Enough!":
  the grave,
  a barren womb,
  a land that never gets enough water,
  a fire that does not say, "Enough!"

30:15b-16

Marriage

Three things are too amazing to me,
even four that I cannot understand:
  an eagle making its way through the sky,
  a snake making its way over a rock,
  a ship making its way through high seas,
  a man making his way with a virgin.

30:18-19

This is the way of a woman who commits adultery:
  She eats, wipes her mouth,
    and says, "I haven't done anything wrong!"

30:20

Three things cause the earth to tremble,
even four it cannot bear up under:
  a slave when he becomes king,
  a godless fool when he is filled with food,
  a woman who is unloved when she gets married,
  a maid when she replaces her mistress.

30:21-23

Who can find a wife with a strong character?
She is worth far more than jewels.
Her husband trusts her with ⌊all⌋ his heart,
  and he does not lack anything good.
She helps him and never harms him all the days of her life. . . .
Her husband is known at the city gates
  when he sits with the leaders of the land. . . .
She keeps a close eye on the conduct of her family,
  and she does not eat the bread of idleness.
Her children and her husband
  stand up and bless her.
In addition, he sings her praises, by saying,
  'Many women have done noble work,
    but you have surpassed them all!'

31:10-12,23,27-29

NATIONAL CONCERNS AND LEADERSHIP

A nation is only as good as the people within it. That's why we need to seek God's direction for establishing a godly nation and leadership. His Word has plenty to say about it. We need to pay attention.

So walk in the way of good people
and stay on the paths of righteous people.
Decent people will live in the land.
People of integrity will remain in it.
But wicked people will be cut off from the land
and treacherous people will be torn from it.

2:20-22

I, Wisdom, live with insight,
and I acquire knowledge and foresight.
To fear the LORD is to hate evil.
I hate pride, arrogance, evil behavior, and twisted speech.
Advice and priceless wisdom are mine.
I, Understanding, have strength.
Through me kings reign,
and rulers decree fair laws.
Through me princes rule,
so do nobles and all fair judges.

8:12-16

A large population is an honor for a king,
but without people a ruler is ruined. . . .
Righteousness lifts up a nation,
but sin is a disgrace in any society.
A king is delighted with a servant who acts wisely,
but he is furious with one who acts shamefully.

14:28,34-35

When a person's ways are pleasing to the LORD,
he makes even his enemies to be at peace with him.

16:7

When a divine revelation is on a king's lips,
he cannot voice a wrong judgment.

16:10

Wrongdoing is disgusting to kings
  because a throne is established through righteousness.
Kings are happy with honest words,
  and whoever speaks what is right is loved.
A king's anger announces death,
  but a wise man makes peace with him.
When the king is cheerful, there is life,
  and his favor is like a cloud bringing spring rain.

16:12-15

A gift opens doors for the one who gives it
  and brings him into the presence of great people. . . .
Flipping a coin ends quarrels
  and settles ⌊issues⌋ between powerful people.

18:16,18

Luxury does not fit a fool,
  much less a slave ruling princes.

19:10

The rage of a king is like the roar of a lion,
  but his favor is like dew on the grass.

19:12

The rage of a king is like the roar of a lion.
  Whoever makes him angry forfeits his life. . . .
A king who sits on his throne to judge
    sifts out every evil with his eyes.

20:2,8

A wise king scatters the wicked
  and then runs them over. . . .
Mercy and truth protect a king,
  and with mercy he maintains his throne.

20:26,28

The king's heart is like streams of water.
Both are under the LORD's control.
He turns them in any direction he chooses. . . .
No wisdom, no understanding, and no advice
⌊can stand up⌋ against the LORD.
The horse is made ready for the day of battle,
but the victory belongs to the LORD.

21:1,30-31

Drive out a mocker, and conflict will leave.
Quarreling and abuse will stop.
Whoever loves a pure heart and whoever speaks graciously
has a king as his friend.
The LORD's eyes watch over knowledge,
but he overturns the words of a treacherous person.

22:10-12

Do not rob the poor because they are poor
or trample on the rights of an oppressed person
at the city gate,
because the LORD will plead their case
and will take the lives of those who rob them.

22:22-23

Do not move an ancient boundary marker
that your ancestors set in place.
Do you see a person who is efficient in his work?
He will serve kings.
He will not serve unknown people.

22:28-29

When you sit down to eat with a ruler,
pay close attention to what is in front of you,
and put a knife to your throat if you have a big appetite.
Do not crave his delicacies,
because this is food that deceives you.

23:1-3

Do not move an ancient boundary marker
  or enter fields that belong to orphans,
    because the one who is responsible for them is strong.
      He will plead their case against you.

23:10-11

A strong man knows how to use his strength,
  but a person with knowledge is even more powerful.
    After all, with the right strategy you can wage war,
      and with many advisers there is victory.

24:5-6

Fear the LORD, my son.
Fear the king as well.
  Do not associate with those who always insist upon change,
    because disaster will come to them suddenly.
      Who knows what misery both may bring?

24:21-22

These also are the sayings of wise people:

Showing partiality as a judge is not good.
  Whoever says to a guilty person, "You are innocent,"
    will be cursed by people and condemned by nations.
  But people will be pleased with those
      who convict a guilty person,
    and a great blessing will come to them.
Giving a straight answer is ⌊like⌋ a kiss on the lips.

24:23-26

It is the glory of God to hide things
  but the glory of kings to investigate them.
⌊Like⌋ the high heavens and the deep earth,
  so the mind of kings is unsearchable.

25:2-3

Take the impurities out of silver,
and a vessel is ready for the silversmith to mold.
Take a wicked person away from the presence of a king,
and justice will make his throne secure.

25:4-5

Do not brag about yourself in front of a king
or stand in the spot that belongs to notable people,
because it is better to be told, "Come up here,"
than to be put down in front of a prince
whom your eyes have seen.

25:6-7

When a country is in revolt, it has many rulers,
but only with a person who has understanding
and knowledge
will it last a long time.

28:2

Those who abandon ⌊God's⌋ teachings praise wicked people,
but those who follow ⌊God's⌋ teachings
oppose wicked people.
Evil people do not understand justice,
but those who seek the LORD understand everything.

28:4-5

When righteous people triumph, there is great glory,
but when wicked people rise, people hide themselves.

28:12

⌊Like⌋ a roaring lion and a charging bear,
⌊so⌋ a wicked ruler is a threat to poor people.
A leader without understanding taxes ⌊his people⌋ heavily,
but those who hate unjust gain will live longer.

28:15-16

When wicked people rise, people hide.
When they die, righteous people increase. . . .
When righteous people increase, the people ⌊of God⌋ rejoice,
but when a wicked person rules, everybody groans.

28:28;29:2

By means of justice, a king builds up a country,
but a person who confiscates religious contributions
tears it down.

29:4

Mockers create an uproar in a city,
but wise people turn away anger. . . .
If a ruler pays attention to lies,
all his servants become wicked.

29:8,12

When a king judges the poor with honesty,
his throne will always be secure. . . .
When wicked people increase, crime increases,
but righteous people will witness their downfall.

29:14,16

Many seek an audience with a ruler,
but justice for humanity comes from the LORD.

29:26

Three things cause the earth to tremble,
even four it cannot bear up under:
a slave when he becomes king,
a godless fool when he is filled with food,
a woman who is unloved when she gets married,
a maid when she replaces her mistress.

30:21-23

There are three things that walk with dignity,
even four that march with dignity:
  a lion, mightiest among animals,
    which turns away from nothing,
  a strutting rooster,
  a male goat,
  a king at the head of his army.

30:29-31

What, my son?
What, son to whom I gave birth?
What, son of my prayers?
  Don't give your strength to women
    or your power to those who ruin kings.

It is not for kings, Lemuel.
It is not for kings to drink wine or for rulers to crave liquor.
  Otherwise, they drink and forget what they have decreed
    and change the standard of justice
      for all oppressed people.
Give liquor to a person who is dying
  and wine to one who feels resentful.
    Such a person drinks
      and forgets his poverty
        and does not remember his trouble anymore.

Speak out for the one who cannot speak,
  for the rights of those who are doomed.
Speak out,
  judge fairly,
    and defend the rights of oppressed and needy people.

31:1-9

OLD AGE

Everywhere we look, we are confronted with potions, powders, and pills to keep us from looking our age. Society teaches us to dread the joy that should come with a lifetime of experiences. These insightful verses exhort us to value the "silver hair" and wisdom we gain.

Old Age

My son,
do not forget my teachings,
and keep my commands in mind,
because they will bring you
long life, good years, and peace. . . .
Long life is in ⌊wisdom's⌋ right hand.
In ⌊wisdom's⌋ left hand are riches and honor.

3:1-2,16

You will live longer because of me,
and years will be added to your life.

9:11

The fear of the LORD lengthens ⌊the number of⌋ days,
but the years of wicked people are shortened.

10:27

Silver hair is a beautiful crown found in a righteous life.

16:31

Grandchildren are the crown of grandparents,
and parents are the glory of their children.

17:6

Listen to advice and accept discipline
so that you may be wise the rest of your life.

19:20

While the glory of young men is their strength,
the splendor of older people is their silver hair.

20:29

Train a child in the way he should go,
and even when he is old he will not turn away from it.

22:6

PARENTING AND DISCIPLINING CHILDREN

Being a parent is one of the most difficult jobs in the world. How wonderful it is that God doesn't neglect this area when the Proverbs admonish us about life. Within these verses are tried and true principles for being the best parents we can be.

Parenting and Disciplining Children

My son,
listen to your father's discipline,
and do not neglect your mother's teachings,
because discipline and teachings
are a graceful garland on your head
and a ⌊golden⌋ chain around your neck.

1:8-9

A wise son makes his father happy,
but a foolish son brings grief to his mother.

10:1

A wise son listens to his father's discipline,
but a mocker does not listen to reprimands. . . .
Whoever refuses to spank his son hates him,
but whoever loves his son disciplines him from early on.

13:1,24

Good people leave an inheritance to their grandchildren,
but the wealth of sinners is stored away for a righteous person.

13:22

A stubborn fool despises his father's discipline,
but whoever appreciates a warning shows good sense. . . .
A wise son makes his father happy,
but a foolish child despises its mother.

15:5,20

Grandchildren are the crown of grandparents,
and parents are the glory of their children.

17:6

The parent of a fool has grief,
and the father of a godless fool has no joy. . . .
A foolish son is a heartache to his father
and bitter grief to his mother.

17:21,25

A foolish son ruins his father,
  and a quarreling woman is like constantly dripping water.

19:13

Discipline your son while there is still hope.
  Do not be the one responsible for his death.

19:18

A son who assaults his father ⌊and⌋ who drives away his mother
  brings shame and disgrace.
If you stop listening to instruction, my son,
  you will stray from the words of knowledge.

19:26-27

A righteous person lives on the basis of his integrity.
  Blessed are his children after he is gone.

20:7

Even a child makes himself known by his actions,
  whether his deeds are pure or right.

20:11

The lamp of the person who curses his father and mother
  will be snuffed out in total darkness.

20:20

An inheritance quickly obtained in the beginning
  will never be blessed in the end.

20:21

Brutal beatings cleanse away wickedness.
Such beatings cleanse the innermost being.

20:30

Train a child in the way he should go,
  and even when he is old he will not turn away from it. . . .
Foolishness is firmly attached to a child's heart.
  Spanking will remove it far from him.

22:6,15

Do not hesitate to discipline a child.
If you spank him, he will not die.
Spank him yourself,
and you will save his soul from hell.

23:13-14

My son,
if you have a wise heart,
my heart will rejoice as well.
My heart rejoices when you speak what is right. . . .
My son,
listen, be wise,
and keep your mind going in the right direction.

23:15-16,19

Listen to your father since you are his son,
and do not despise your mother because she is old.
Buy truth (and do not sell it),
⌊that is,⌋ buy wisdom, discipline, and understanding.
A righteous person's father will certainly rejoice.
Someone who has a wise son will enjoy him.
May your father and your mother be glad.
May she who gave birth to you rejoice.

My son,
give me your heart.
Let your eyes find happiness in my ways.
A prostitute is a deep pit.
A loose woman is a narrow well.
She is like a robber, lying in ambush.
She spreads unfaithfulness throughout society.

23:22-28

Be wise, my son, and make my heart glad
so that I can answer anyone who criticizes me.

27:11

Whoever follows ⌊God's⌋ teachings is a wise son.
Whoever associates with gluttons disgraces his father.

28:7

The one who robs his father or his mother
and says, "It isn't wrong!" is a companion to a vandal.

28:24

A person who loves wisdom makes his father happy,
but one who pays prostitutes wastes his wealth.

29:3

A spanking and a warning produce wisdom,
but an undisciplined child disgraces his mother. . . .
Correct your son, and he will give you peace of mind.
He will bring delight to your soul.

29:15,17

A certain kind of person curses his father
and does not bless his mother. . . .
The eye that makes fun of a father and hates to obey a mother
will be plucked out by ravens in the valley
and eaten by young vultures.

30:11,17

She keeps a close eye on the conduct of her family,
and she does not eat the bread of idleness.
Her children and her husband
stand up and bless her.
In addition, he sings her praises, by saying,
'Many women have done noble work,
but you have surpassed them all!'

31:27-29

PEACE OF MIND

When worry weighs us down, we can take comfort in God's promises that trusting him will bring peace. Within the Proverbs are some of the most powerful "peace-producing" verses of the Bible.

Peace of Mind

Wisdom sings her song in the streets.
In the public squares she raises her voice.
At the corners of noisy streets she calls out.
At the entrances to the city she speaks her words,
"... whoever listens to me will live without worry
and will be free from the dread of disaster."

1:20-21,33

My son,
do not forget my teachings,
and keep my commands in mind,
because they will bring you
long life, good years, and peace.

3:1-2

⌊Wisdom's⌋ ways are pleasant ways,
and all its paths lead to peace.
⌊Wisdom⌋ is a tree of life
for those who take firm hold of it.
Those who cling to it are blessed.

3:17-18

My son,
do not lose sight of these things.
Use priceless wisdom and foresight.
Then they will mean life for you,
and they will grace your neck.
Then you will go safely on your way,
and you will not hurt your foot.
When you lie down, you will not be afraid.
As you lie there, your sleep will be sweet.

Do not be afraid of sudden terror
or of the destruction of wicked people when it comes.
The LORD will be your confidence.
He will keep your foot from getting caught.

3:21-26

That which wicked people dread happens to them,
but ⌊the LORD⌋ grants the desire of righteous people.

10:24

A person's anxiety will weigh him down,
but an encouraging word makes him joyful.
In the fear of the LORD there is strong confidence,
and his children will have a place of refuge.

12:25;14:26

Stubborn fools make fun of guilt,
but there is forgiveness among decent people.

14:9

A tranquil heart makes for a healthy body,
but jealousy is ⌊like⌋ bone cancer.

14:30

A joyful heart makes a cheerful face,
but with a heartache comes depression.

15:13

By mercy and faithfulness, peace is made with the LORD.
By the fear of the LORD, evil is avoided.
When a person's ways are pleasing to the LORD,
he makes even his enemies to be at peace with him.

16:6-7

Better a bite of dry bread ⌊eaten⌋ in peace
than a family feast filled with strife.

17:1

The fear of the LORD leads to life,
and such a person will rest easy without suffering harm.

19:23

Peace of Mind

Do not get overly upset with evildoers.
Do not envy wicked people,
because an evil person has no future,
and the lamps of wicked people will be snuffed out.
24:19-20

Do not brag about tomorrow,
because you do not know what another day may bring.
27:1

When a wise person goes to court with a stubborn fool,
he may rant and rave,
but there is no peace and quiet.
29:9

Correct your son, and he will give you peace of mind.
He will bring delight to your soul.
29:17

She does not fear for her family when it snows
because her whole family
has a double layer of clothing.
31:21

She dresses with strength and nobility,
and she smiles at the future.
31:25

PLANS AND GOALS

Plans are easy to make; the challenge is to bring them into alignment with God's intentions and desires for the benefit of the whole world. We find from the following wise sayings that God will have his way, whether or not we go along with his ideas. It's a good thing our feeble perspective can't sway God's purposes.

The Lord gives wisdom.
From his mouth come knowledge and understanding.
He has reserved priceless wisdom for decent people.
He is a shield for those who walk in integrity
in order to guard those on paths of justice
and to watch over the way of his godly ones.
Then you will understand what is right and just and fair—
every good course ⌊in life⌋.

2:6-9

Trust the Lord with all your heart,
and do not rely on your own understanding.
In all your ways acknowledge him,
and he will make your paths smooth.

3:5-6

Do not plan to do something wrong to your neighbor
while he is sitting there with you and suspecting nothing.

3:29

Consider the ant, you lazy bum.
Watch its ways, and become wise.
Although it has no overseer, officer, or ruler,
in summertime it stores its food supply.
At harvest time it gathers its food.

How long will you lie there, you lazy bum?
When will you get up from your sleep?
"Just a little sleep,
just a little slumber,
just a little nap."
Then your poverty will come ⌊to you⌋ like a drifter,
and your need will come ⌊to you⌋ like a bandit.

6:6-11

There are six things that the Lord hates,
even seven that are disgusting to him:

arrogant eyes,
a lying tongue,
hands that kill innocent people,
a mind devising wicked plans,
feet that are quick to do wrong,
a dishonest witness spitting out lies,
and a person who spreads conflict among relatives.

6:16-19

It is the LORD's blessing that makes a person rich,
and hard work adds nothing to it.

10:22

A nation will fall when there is no direction,
but with many advisers there is victory.

11:14

Deceit is in the heart of those who plan evil,
but joy belongs to those who advise peace.

12:20

Delayed hope makes one sick at heart,
but a fulfilled longing is a tree of life.

13:12

The wisest of women builds up her home,
but a stupid one tears it down with her own hands.

14:1

The wisdom of a sensible person guides his way of life,
but the stupidity of fools misleads them.

14:8

There is a way that seems right to a person,
but eventually it ends in death. . . .
A heart that turns ⌊from God⌋ becomes bored with its own ways,
but a good person is satisfied with God's ways.

14:12,14

A short-tempered person acts stupidly,
and a person who plots evil is hated. . . .
Don't those who stray plan what is evil,
while those who are merciful and faithful
plan what is good?

14:17,22

The way of wicked people is disgusting to the LORD,
but he loves those who pursue righteousness. . . .
The path of lazy people is like a thorny hedge,
but the road of decent people is an ⌊open⌋ highway.

15:9,19

Without advice plans go wrong,
but with many advisers they succeed.

15:22

The path of life for a wise person leads upward
in order to turn him away from hell below.

15:24

The plans of the heart belong to humans,
but an answer on the tongue comes from the LORD.

16:1

Entrust your efforts to the LORD,
and your plans will succeed.
The LORD has made everything for his own purpose,
even wicked people for the day of trouble. . . .
A person may plan his own journey,
but the LORD directs his steps.

16:3-4,9

When a divine revelation is on a king's lips,
he cannot voice a wrong judgment.

16:10

There is a way that seems right to a person,
but eventually it ends in death.

16:25

A worthless person plots trouble,
and his speech is like a burning fire. . . .
Whoever winks his eye is plotting something devious.
Whoever bites his lips has finished his evil work.

16:27,30

The dice are thrown,
but the LORD determines every outcome.

16:33

A person without knowledge is no good.
A person in a hurry makes mistakes.
The stupidity of a person turns his life upside down,
and his heart rages against the LORD. . . .
Many plans are in the human heart,
but the advice of the LORD will endure.

19:2-3,21

A lazy person does not plow in the fall.
He looks for something in the harvest but finds nothing.

20:4

A motive in the human heart is like deep water,
and a person who has understanding draws it out. . . .
Even a child makes himself known by his actions,
whether his deeds are pure or right.

20:5,11

Plans are confirmed by getting advice,
and with guidance one wages war.

20:18

The LORD is the one who directs a person's steps.
How then can anyone understand his own way?

20:24

The king's heart is like streams of water.
Both are under the LORD's control.
He turns them in any direction he chooses.

21:1

The plans of a hard-working person lead to prosperity,
but everyone who is ⌊always⌋ in a hurry ends up in poverty.

21:5

No wisdom, no understanding, and no advice
⌊can stand up⌋ against the LORD.
The horse is made ready for the day of battle,
but the victory belongs to the LORD.

21:30-31

Do you see a person who is efficient in his work?
He will serve kings.
He will not serve unknown people.

22:29

A strong man knows how to use his strength,
but a person with knowledge is even more powerful.
After all, with the right strategy you can wage war,
and with many advisers there is victory.

24:5-6

Whoever plans to do evil will be known as a schemer.
Foolish scheming is sinful,
and a mocker is disgusting to everyone.

24:8-9

You wicked one,
do not lie in ambush at the home of a righteous person.
Do not rob his house.

24:15

Do not get overly upset with evildoers.
Do not envy wicked people,
because an evil person has no future,
and the lamps of wicked people will be snuffed out.

24:19-20

Prepare your work outside,
and get things ready for yourself in the field.
Afterwards, build your house. . . .
I passed by a lazy person's field,
the vineyard belonging to a person without sense.
I saw that it was all overgrown with thistles.
The ground was covered with weeds,
and its stone fence was torn down.
When I observed ⌊this⌋, I took it to heart.
I saw it and learned my lesson.
"Just a little sleep,
just a little slumber,
just a little nap."
Then your poverty will come like a drifter,
and your need will come like a bandit.

24:27,30-34

Do not brag about tomorrow,
because you do not know what another day may bring.

27:1

Whoever works his land will have plenty to eat.
Whoever chases unrealistic dreams will have
plenty of nothing.

A trustworthy person has many blessings,
but anyone in a hurry to get rich
will not escape punishment. . . .
A stingy person is in a hurry to get rich,
not realizing that poverty is about to overtake him.

28:19-20,22

Who can find a wife with a strong character?
She is worth far more than jewels.
Her husband trusts her with ⌊all⌋ his heart,
and he does not lack anything good.
She helps him and never harms him all the days of her life.

She seeks out wool and linen ⌊with care⌋
and works with willing hands.
She is like merchant ships.
She brings her food from far away.
She wakes up while it is still dark
and gives food to her family
and portions of food to her female slaves.

She picks out a field and buys it.
She plants a vineyard from the profits she has earned.
She puts on strength like a belt
and goes to work with energy.
She sees that she is making a good profit.
Her lamp burns late at night.

She puts her hands on the distaff,
and her fingers hold a spindle.
She opens her hands to oppressed people
and stretches them out to needy people.
She does not fear for her family when it snows
because her whole family
has a double layer of clothing.
She makes quilts for herself.
Her clothes are ⌊made of⌋ linen and purple cloth.

Her husband is known at the city gates
when he sits with the leaders of the land.

She makes linen garments and sells them
and delivers belts to the merchants.
She dresses with strength and nobility,
and she smiles at the future.

She speaks with wisdom,
  and on her tongue there is tender instruction.
She keeps a close eye on the conduct of her family,
  and she does not eat the bread of idleness.
Her children and her husband
  stand up and bless her.
In addition, he sings her praises, by saying,
  'Many women have done noble work,
    but you have surpassed them all!'

Charm is deceptive, and beauty evaporates,
  ⌊but⌋ a woman who has the fear of the LORD
      should be praised.
Reward her for what she has done,
  and let her achievements praise her at the city gates.

31:10-31

PRAYER

Prayer is a two-way conversation with God that produces a difference in our lives. The wisdom of the Proverbs has something to say about this important part of our walk with God.

A sacrifice brought by wicked people is disgusting to the LORD,
but the prayers of decent people please him.

15:8

The LORD is far from wicked people,
but he hears the prayers of righteous people.

15:29

The name of the LORD is a strong tower.
A righteous person runs to it and is safe.

18:10

Surely the prayer of someone who refuses
to listen to ⌊God's⌋ teachings is disgusting.

28:9

Whoever covers over his sins does not prosper.
Whoever confesses and abandons them receives compassion.

28:13

This man's declaration:
"I'm weary, O God.
I'm weary and worn out, O God.
I'm more ⌊like⌋ a dumb animal than a human being.
I don't ⌊even⌋ have human understanding.
I haven't learned wisdom.
I don't have knowledge of the Holy One. . . .

"I've asked you for two things.
Don't keep them from me before I die:
Keep vanity and lies far away from me.
Don't give me either poverty or riches.
Feed me ⌊only⌋ the food I need,
or I may feel satisfied and deny you
and say, 'Who is the LORD?'
or I may become poor and steal
and give the name of my God a bad reputation."

30:1-3, 7-9

PRIDE AND HUMILITY

If pride is having an inflated view of oneself, then humility is thinking the truth about oneself. However, humility also acknowledges the talents, gifts, and insight God has given us. The Proverbs help us judge ourselves correctly.

Do not consider yourself wise.
Fear the LORD, and turn away from evil.
⌊Then⌋ your body will be healed,
and your bones will have nourishment.

3:7-8

The LORD curses the house of wicked people,
but he blesses the home of righteous people.
When he mocks the mockers,
he is gracious to humble people.
Wise people will inherit honor,
but fools will bear disgrace.

3:33-35

My son,
if you guarantee a loan for your neighbor
or pledge yourself for a stranger with a handshake,
you are trapped by the words of your own mouth,
caught by your own promise.

Do the following things, my son,
so that you may free yourself,
because you have fallen into your neighbor's hands:
Humble yourself,
and pester your neighbor.
Don't let your eyes rest
or your eyelids close.
Free yourself like a gazelle from the hand of a hunter
and like a bird from the hand of a hunter.

6:1-5

There are six things that the LORD hates,
even seven that are disgusting to him:
arrogant eyes,
a lying tongue,
hands that kill innocent people,
a mind devising wicked plans,
feet that are quick to do wrong,

a dishonest witness spitting out lies,
and a person who spreads conflict among relatives.
6:16-19

I, Wisdom, live with insight,
and I acquire knowledge and foresight.
To fear the LORD is to hate evil.
I hate pride, arrogance, evil behavior, and twisted speech.
8:12-13

Arrogance comes,
then comes shame,
but wisdom remains with humble people.
11:2

Better to be unimportant and have a slave
than to act important and have nothing to eat.
12:9

One person pretends to be rich but has nothing.
Another pretends to be poor but has great wealth. . . .
Arrogance produces only quarreling,
but those who take advice gain wisdom.
13:7,10

A wise person is cautious and turns away from evil,
but a fool is careless and overconfident. . . .
In the fear of the LORD there is strong confidence,
and his children will have a place of refuge.
14:16,26

The LORD tears down the house of an arrogant person,
but he protects the property of widows. . . .
The fear of the LORD is discipline ⌊leading to⌋ wisdom,
and humility comes before honor.
15:25,33

Everyone with a conceited heart is disgusting to the LORD.
  Certainly, ⌊such a person⌋ will not go unpunished. . . .
Pride precedes a disaster,
  and an arrogant attitude precedes a fall.
Better to be humble with lowly people
  than to share stolen goods with arrogant people.

16:5,18-19

Before destruction a person's heart is arrogant,
  but humility comes before honor.

18:12

Who can say,
  "I've made my heart pure.
  I'm cleansed from my sin"?

20:9

A conceited look and an arrogant attitude,
  which are the lamps of wicked people, are sins. . . .
An arrogant, conceited person is called a mocker.
  His arrogance knows no limits.

21:4,24

On the heels of humility (the fear of the LORD)
  are riches and honor and life.

22:4

Do not be happy when your enemy falls,
  and do not feel glad when he stumbles.
    The LORD will see it, he won't like it,
      and he will turn his anger away from that person.

24:17-18

Do not brag about yourself in front of a king
  or stand in the spot that belongs to notable people,
    because it is better to be told, "Come up here,"
      than to be put down in front of a prince
        whom your eyes have seen.

25:6-7

⌊Like⌋ a dense fog or a dust storm,
⌊so⌋ is a person who brags about a gift that he does not give. . . .
Eating too much honey is not good,
and searching for honor is not honorable.

25:14,27

Like snow in summertime and rain at harvest time,
so honor is not right for a fool. . . .
Like tying a stone to a sling,
so is giving honor to a fool. . . .
Have you met a person who thinks he is wise?
There is more hope for a fool than for him.

26:1,8,12

Do not brag about tomorrow,
because you do not know what another day may bring.

27:1

Praise should come from another person
and not from your own mouth,
from a stranger and not from your own lips. . . .
The crucible is for refining silver and the smelter for gold,
but a person ⌊is tested⌋ by the praise given to him.

27:2,21

As a face is reflected in water,
so a person is reflected by his heart.

27:19

A rich person is wise in his own eyes,
but a poor person with understanding
sees right through him. . . .
Whoever covers over his sins does not prosper.
Whoever confesses and abandons them receives compassion.

28:11,13

A person who will not bend after many warnings
will suddenly be broken beyond repair. . . .
A person's pride will humiliate him,
but a humble spirit gains honor.

29:1,23

This man's declaration:
"I'm weary, O God.
I'm weary and worn out, O God.
I'm more ⌊like⌋ a dumb animal than a human being.
I don't ⌊even⌋ have human understanding.
I haven't learned wisdom.
I don't have knowledge of the Holy One."

30:1b-3

A certain kind of person thinks he is pure
but is not washed from his own feces.
A certain kind of person looks around arrogantly
and is conceited.

30:12-13

If you are such a godless fool as to honor yourself,
or if you scheme,
you had better put your hand over your mouth.

30:32

RELATIONSHIPS WITHIN THE COMMUNITY

Unless we're trapped alone on an island, we're destined to face the challenge of interacting with people. God's Word doesn't leave us without some insights into making our world, especially our communities, a place where we can invest ourselves.

Do not hold back anything good
from those who are entitled to it
when you have the power to do so.
When you have the good thing with you,
do not tell your neighbor,
"Go away!
Come back tomorrow.
I'll give you something then."

Do not plan to do something wrong to your neighbor
while he is sitting there with you and suspecting nothing.
Do not quarrel with a person for no reason
if he has not harmed you.

3:27-30

My son,
if you guarantee a loan for your neighbor
or pledge yourself for a stranger with a handshake,
you are trapped by the words of your own mouth,
caught by your own promise.

Do the following things, my son,
so that you may free yourself,
because you have fallen into your neighbor's hands:
Humble yourself,
and pester your neighbor.
Don't let your eyes rest
or your eyelids close.
Free yourself like a gazelle from the hand of a hunter
and like a bird from the hand of a hunter.

6:1-5

With his talk a godless person can ruin his neighbor,
but righteous people are rescued by knowledge.

11:9

When righteous people prosper, a city is glad.
When wicked people die, there are songs of joy.
With the blessing of decent people a city is raised up,
but by the words of wicked people, it is torn down.

11:10-11

A person who despises a neighbor has no sense,
but a person who has understanding keeps quiet. . . .
A nation will fall when there is no direction,
but with many advisers there is victory. . . .
Whoever guarantees a stranger's loan will get into trouble,
but whoever hates the closing of a deal remains secure.

11:12,14-15

A righteous person looks out for his neighbor,
but the path of wicked people leads others astray.

12:26

The houses of wicked people will be destroyed,
but the tents of decent people will continue to expand.

14:11

A poor person is hated even by his neighbor,
but a rich person is loved by many.
Whoever despises his neighbor sins,
but blessed is the one who is kind to humble people.

14:20-21

A large population is an honor for a king,
but without people a ruler is ruined.

14:28

Righteousness lifts up a nation,
but sin is a disgrace in any society.
A king is delighted with a servant who acts wisely,
but he is furious with one who acts shamefully.

14:34-35

When a person's ways are pleasing to the LORD,
he makes even his enemies to be at peace with him.
16:7

A friend always loves,
and a brother is born to share trouble.
17:17

Flipping a coin ends quarrels
and settles ⌊issues⌋ between powerful people.
An offended brother is more ⌊resistant⌋ than a strong city,
and disputes are like the locked gate of a castle tower.
18:18-19

The mind of a wicked person desires evil
and has no consideration for his neighbor.
21:10

Do not move an ancient boundary marker
that your ancestors set in place. . . .
Do not move an ancient boundary marker
or enter fields that belong to orphans,
because the one who is responsible for them is strong.
He will plead their case against you.
22:28;23:10-11

Do not be in a hurry to go to court.
What will you do in the end if your neighbor disgraces you?
Present your argument to your neighbor,
but do not reveal another person's secret.
Otherwise, when he hears about it,
he will humiliate you,
and his evil report about you will never disappear.
25:8-10

Do not set foot in your neighbor's house too often.
  Otherwise, he will see too much of you and hate you.

25:17

⌊Like⌋ grabbing a dog by the ears,
  ⌊so⌋ is a bystander who gets involved in someone else's quarrel.
Like a madman who shoots flaming arrows, arrows, and death,
  so is the person who tricks his neighbor
    and says, "I was only joking!"

26:17-19

A stone is heavy, and sand weighs a lot,
  but annoyance caused by a stubborn fool
    is heavier than both. . . .
Do not abandon your friend or your father's friend.
Do not go to a relative's home when you are in trouble.
  A neighbor living nearby is better than a relative far away.

27:3,10

Whoever blesses his friend early in the morning
    with a loud voice—
  his blessing is considered a curse.

27:14

When wicked people increase, crime increases,
  but righteous people will witness their downfall.

29:16

SELF EXAMINATION

God's Word is clear. We need to evaluate our growth, or lack of it, in order to become more of who God wants us to be. It's not always a pleasant revelation, but the results can be attractive if we're willing to make changes.

Self Examination

Who can say,
"I've made my heart pure.
I'm cleansed from my sin"?

20:9

It is a trap for a person to say impulsively,
"This is a holy offering!"
and later to have second thoughts about those vows.

20:25

A person thinks everything he does is right,
but the LORD weighs hearts.

21:2

A wicked person puts up a bold front,
but a decent person's way of life is his own security.

21:29

As a dog goes back to its vomit,
⌊so⌋ a fool repeats his stupidity.

26:11

Whoever covers over his sins does not prosper.
Whoever confesses and abandons them receives compassion.

28:13

Blessed is the one who is always fearful ⌊of sin⌋,
but whoever is hard-hearted falls into disaster.

28:14

A certain kind of person thinks he is pure
but is not washed from his own feces.
A certain kind of person looks around arrogantly
and is conceited.

30:12-13

SEXUAL SINS, ADULTERY, AND TEMPTATION

In times of temptation, we need God's Word to help us resist our human passions. Adultery, unfortunately, is one of those pitfalls that can seem attractive, yet as the Proverbs in this section demonstrate, we'll only experience heartache if we succumb to its lure.

⌊Wisdom will⌋ also save you
from an adulterous woman,
from a loose woman with her smooth talk,
who leaves ⌊her husband,⌋
the closest friend of her youth,
and forgets her marriage vows to her God.
Her house sinks down to death.
Her ways lead to the souls of the dead.
None who have sex with her come back.
Nor do they ever reach the paths of life.

So walk in the way of good people
and stay on the paths of righteous people.
Decent people will live in the land.
People of integrity will remain in it.
But wicked people will be cut off from the land
and treacherous people will be torn from it.

2:16-22

My son,
pay attention to my wisdom.
Open your ears to my understanding
so that you may act with foresight
and speak with insight.

The lips of an adulterous woman drip with honey.
Her kiss is smoother than oil,
but in the end she is as bitter as wormwood,
as sharp as a two-edged sword.
Her feet descend to death.
Her steps lead straight to hell.
She doesn't even think about the path of life.
Her steps wander, and she doesn't realize it.

But now, sons,
listen to me,
and do not turn away from what I say to you.

Stay far away from her.
Do not even go near her door.
  Either you will surrender your reputation to others
    and ⌊the rest of⌋ your years to some cruel person,
  or strangers will benefit from your strength
    and you will have to work hard in a pagan's house.
  Then you will groan when your end comes,
    when your body and flesh are consumed.
  You will say,
    "Oh, how I hated discipline!
    How my heart despised correction!
      I didn't listen to what my teachers said to me,
        nor did I keep my ear open to my instructors.
      I almost reached total ruin
        in the assembly and in the congregation."

Drink water out of your own cistern
  and running water from your own well.
    Why should water flow out of your spring?
    Why should your streams flow into the streets?
      They should be yours alone,
        so do not share them with strangers.
Let your own fountain be blessed,
  and enjoy the girl you married when you were young,
    a loving doe and a graceful deer.
  Always let her breasts satisfy you.
  Always be intoxicated with her love.
    Why should you, my son,
      be intoxicated with an adulterous woman
        and fondle a loose woman's breast?

Each person's ways are clearly seen by the LORD,
  and he surveys all his actions.
A wicked person will be trapped by his own wrongs,
  and he will be caught in the ropes of his own sin.
He will die for his lack of discipline
  and stumble around because of his great stupidity.

5:1-23

Sexual Sins, Adultery, and Temptation

My son,
obey the command of your father,
and do not disregard the teachings of your mother.
Fasten them on your heart forever.
Hang them around your neck.
When you walk around, they will lead you.
When you lie down, they will watch over you.
When you wake up, they will talk to you
because the command is a lamp,
the teachings are a light,
and the warnings from discipline
are the path of life
to keep you from an evil woman
and from the smooth talk of a loose woman.

Do not desire her beauty in your heart.
Do not let her catch you with her eyes.
A prostitute's price is ⌊only⌋ a loaf of bread,
but a married woman hunts for ⌊your⌋ life itself.
Can a man carry fire in his lap
without burning his clothes?
Can anyone walk on red-hot coals
without burning his feet?
So it is with a man who has sex with his neighbor's wife.
None who touch her will escape punishment.
People do not despise a thief who is hungry
when he steals to satisfy his appetite,
but when he is caught,
he has to repay it seven times.
He must give up all the possessions in his house.

Whoever commits adultery with a woman has no sense.
Whoever does this destroys himself.
An adulterous man will find disease and dishonor,
and his disgrace will not be blotted out,

because jealousy arouses a husband's fury.
The husband will show no mercy
when he takes revenge.
No amount of money will change his mind.
The largest bribe will not satisfy him.

6:20-35

My son,
pay attention to my words.
Treasure my commands that are within you.
Obey my commands so that you may live.
Follow my teachings just as you protect
the pupil of your eye.
Tie them on your fingers.
Write them on the tablet of your heart.
Say to wisdom, "You are my sister."
Give the name "my relative" to understanding
in order to guard yourself from an adulterous woman,
from a loose woman with her smooth talk.

From a window in my house I looked through my screen.
I was looking at gullible people
when I saw a young man without much sense
among youths.
He was crossing a street near her corner
and walking toward her house
in the twilight,
in the evening,
in the dark hours of the night.

A woman with an ulterior motive meets him.
She is dressed as a prostitute.
She is loud and rebellious.
Her feet will not stay at home.
One moment she is out on the street,
the next she is at the curb,
on the prowl at every corner.

She grabs him and kisses him and brazenly says to him,
"I have some sacrificial meat.
Today I kept my vows.
That's why I came to meet you.
Eagerly, I looked for you,
and I've found you.
I've made my bed,
with colored sheets of Egyptian linen.
I've sprinkled my bed with myrrh, aloes, and cinnamon.
Come, let's drink our fill of love until morning.
Let's enjoy making love,
because my husband's not home.
He has gone on a long trip.
He took lots of money with him.
He won't be home for a couple of weeks."

With all her seductive charms, she persuades him.
With her smooth lips, she makes him give in.
He immediately follows her
like a steer on its way to be slaughtered,
like a ram hobbling into captivity
until an arrow pierces his heart,
like a bird darting into a trap.
He does not realize that it will cost him his life.

Now, sons,
listen to me.
Pay attention to the words from my mouth.
Do not let your heart be turned to her ways.
Do not wander onto her paths,
because she has brought down many victims,
and she has killed all too many.
Her home is the way to hell
and leads to the darkest vaults of death.

7:1-27

The woman Stupidity is loud, gullible, and ignorant.
She sits at the doorway of her house.
She is enthroned on the high ground of the city
 and calls to those who pass by,
  those minding their own business,
   "Whoever is gullible turn in here!"

She says to a person without sense,
 "Stolen waters are sweet,
  and food eaten in secret is tasty."
But he does not know
 that the souls of the dead are there,
 that her guests are in the depths of hell.

9:13-18

The mouth of an adulterous woman is a deep pit.
 The one who is cursed by the LORD will fall into it.

22:14

My son,
 give me your heart.
 Let your eyes find happiness in my ways.
  A prostitute is a deep pit.
  A loose woman is a narrow well.
  She is like a robber, lying in ambush.
  She spreads unfaithfulness throughout society.

23:26-28

One who is full despises honey,
 but to one who is hungry,
  even bitter food tastes sweet.
Like a bird wandering from its nest,
 so is a husband wandering from his home.

27:7-8

A person who loves wisdom makes his father happy,
 but one who pays prostitutes wastes his wealth.

29:3

This is the way of a woman who commits adultery:
She eats, wipes her mouth,
and says, "I haven't done anything wrong!"

30:20

Don't give your strength to women
or your power to those who ruin kings.

31:3

STRENGTH, SECURITY, AND CONFIDENCE

We all want to be the kind of person who doesn't let life get us down. Strength means viewing life from God's perspective, and the insights of the Proverbs provide ideas for responding to life's hazards, trusting that God is truly in control.

Trust the LORD with all your heart,
and do not rely on your own understanding.
In all your ways acknowledge him,
and he will make your paths smooth.
Do not consider yourself wise.
Fear the LORD, and turn away from evil.
⌊Then⌋ your body will be healed,
and your bones will have nourishment.

3:5-8

My son,
listen and accept my words,
and they will multiply the years of your life.
I have taught you the way of wisdom.
I have guided you along decent paths.
When you walk, your stride will not be hampered.
Even if you run, you will not stumble.

4:10-12

A righteous person will never be moved,
but wicked people will not continue to live in the land.

10:30

At the death of a wicked person, hope vanishes.
Moreover, his confidence in strength vanishes.

11:7

A person cannot stand firm on a foundation of wickedness,
and the roots of righteous people cannot be moved.

12:3

A wife with strength of character is the crown of her husband,
but the wife who disgraces him is like bone cancer.

12:4

Where there are no cattle, the feeding trough is empty,
but the strength of an ox produces plentiful harvests.

14:4

In the fear of the LORD there is strong confidence,
  and his children will have a place of refuge.

14:26

While the glory of young men is their strength,
  the splendor of older people is their silver hair.

20:29

A wise man attacks a city of warriors
  and pulls down the strong defenses in which they trust.

21:22

A wicked person puts up a bold front,
  but a decent person's way of life is his own security.

21:29

Do not move an ancient boundary marker
  or enter fields that belong to orphans,
    because the one who is responsible for them is strong.
      He will plead their case against you.

23:10-11

A strong man knows how to use his strength,
  but a person with knowledge is even more powerful.
    After all, with the right strategy you can wage war,
      and with many advisers there is victory.

24:5-6

If you faint in a crisis, you are weak.

24:10

You wicked one,
  do not lie in ambush at the home of a righteous person.
  Do not rob his house.
    A righteous person may fall seven times,
        but he gets up again.
      However, in a disaster wicked people fall.

24:15-16

With patience you can persuade a ruler,
and a soft tongue can break bones.

25:15

⌊Like⌋ a muddied spring and a polluted well,
⌊so⌋ is a righteous person who gives in to a wicked person. . . .
⌊Like⌋ a city broken into ⌊and⌋ left without a wall,
⌊so⌋ is a person who lacks self-control.

25:26,28

A wicked person flees when no one is chasing him,
but righteous people are as bold as lions.

28:1

A person who will not bend after many warnings
will suddenly be broken beyond repair.

29:1

Every word of God has proven to be true.
He is a shield to those who come to him for protection.

30:5

Four things on earth are small,
yet they are very wise:
Ants are not a strong species,
yet they store their food in summer.
Rock badgers are not a mighty species,
yet they make their home in the rocks.
Locusts have no king,
yet all of them divide into swarms by instinct.
A lizard you can hold in your hands,
yet it can even be found in royal palaces.

30:24-28

There are three things that walk with dignity,
even four that march with dignity:
a lion, mightiest among animals,
which turns away from nothing,
a strutting rooster,
a male goat,
a king at the head of his army.

30:29-31

What, my son?
What, son to whom I gave birth?
What, son of my prayers?
Don't give your strength to women
or your power to those who ruin kings.

31:2-3

Speak out for the one who cannot speak,
for the rights of those who are doomed.
Speak out,
judge fairly,
and defend the rights of oppressed and needy people.

31:8-9

Who can find a wife with a strong character?
She is worth far more than jewels.
Her husband trusts her with ⌊all⌋ his heart,
and he does not lack anything good. . . .
She puts on strength like a belt
and goes to work with energy.
She sees that she is making a good profit.
Her lamp burns late at night. . . .
She does not fear for her family when it snows
because her whole family
has a double layer of clothing. . . .
She dresses with strength and nobility,
and she smiles at the future. . . .

Charm is deceptive, and beauty evaporates,
⌊but⌋ a woman who has the fear of the LORD
should be praised.
Reward her for what she has done,
and let her achievements praise her at the city gates.

31:10-11,17-18,21,25,30-31

SUCCESS AND FAILURE

If we follow God's path, he will reward us. Some of these rewards may be earthly happiness, prosperity, and success. But the ultimate reward is the eternal life our Father has promised to us. In times of struggle and failure, we need to remember that God's mercy has provided us with this gift.

Do not let mercy and truth leave you.
Fasten them around your neck.
Write them on the tablet of your heart.
  Then you will find favor and much success
    in the sight of God and humanity.

3:3-4

Sons,
  listen to ⌊your⌋ father's discipline,
    and pay attention in order to gain understanding.
      After all, I have taught you well.
  Do not abandon my teachings.
  When I was a boy ⌊learning⌋ from my father,
  when I was a tender and only child of my mother,
    they used to teach me and say to me,
      "Cling to my words wholeheartedly.
      Obey my commands so that you may live.
      Acquire wisdom.
      Acquire understanding.
      Do not forget.
      Do not turn away from the words that I have spoken.
      Do not abandon wisdom, and it will watch over you.
      Love wisdom, and it will protect you.
        The beginning of wisdom is to acquire wisdom.
        Acquire understanding with all that you have.
        Cherish wisdom.
          It will raise you up.
          It will bring you honor when you embrace it.
          It will give you a graceful garland for your head.
          It will hand you a beautiful crown."

4:1-9

But the path of righteous people is like the light of dawn
  that becomes brighter and brighter until it reaches midday.
The way of wicked people is like deep darkness.
They do not know what makes them stumble.

4:18-19

My son,
  pay attention to my words.
  Open your ears to what I say.
  Do not lose sight of these things.
  Keep them deep within your heart
    because they are life to those who find them
      and they heal the whole body.
  Guard your heart more than anything else,
    because the source of your life flows from it.

4:20-23

Now, sons, listen to me.
  Blessed are those who follow my ways.
    Listen to discipline, and become wise.
    Do not leave my ways.
  Blessed is the person who listens to me,
    watches at my door day after day,
      and waits by my doorposts.
  Whoever finds me finds life
    and obtains favor from the LORD.
  Whoever sins against me harms himself.
  All those who hate me love death.

8:32-36

The name of a righteous person remains blessed,
  but the names of wicked people will rot away.

10:7

A righteous person's reward is life.
A wicked person's harvest is sin.

10:16

The righteousness of innocent people makes their road smooth,
  but wicked people fall by their own wickedness.

11:5

No ⌊lasting⌋ harm comes to a righteous person,
but wicked people have lots of trouble.

12:21

Whoever pursues righteousness and mercy
will find life, righteousness, and honor.

21:21

Eat honey, my son, because it is good.
Honey that flows from the honeycomb tastes sweet.
The knowledge of wisdom is like that for your soul.
If you find it, then there is a future,
and your hope will never be cut off.

24:13-14

TRUSTING GOD AND THE FEAR OF THE LORD

It all boils down to trusting God. When we do, life doesn't seem so overwhelming, and we can respond to life situations in a godly manner. When we don't we can become crushed with fear and depression. We're fortunate that God gives us the Proverbs to show us reasons to trust God.

Trusting God and the Fear of the Lord

The fear of the LORD is the beginning of knowledge.
Stubborn fools despise wisdom and discipline.

1:7

Wisdom sings her song in the streets.
In the public squares she raises her voice.
At the corners of noisy streets she calls out.
At the entrances to the city she speaks her words,
"How long will you gullible people
love being so gullible?
How long will you mockers find joy in your mocking?
How long will you fools hate knowledge?

"Turn to me when I warn you.
I will generously pour out my spirit for you.
I will make my words known to you.

"I called, and you refused to listen.
I stretched out my hands to you,
and no one paid attention.
You ignored all my advice.
You did not want me to warn you.
I will laugh at your calamity.
I will make fun of you
when panic strikes you,
when panic strikes you like a violent storm,
when calamity strikes you like a wind storm,
when trouble and anguish come to you.

"They will call to me at that time, but I will not answer.
They will look for me, but they will not find me,
because they hated knowledge
and did not choose the fear of the LORD."

1:20-29

My son,
if you take my words ⌊to heart⌋
and treasure my commands within you,

if you pay close attention to wisdom,
  and let your mind reach for understanding,
if indeed you call out for insight,
if you ask aloud for understanding,
if you search for wisdom as if it were money
  and hunt for it as if it were hidden treasure,
then you will understand the fear of the LORD
  and you will find the knowledge of God.

2:1-5

Trust the LORD with all your heart,
  and do not rely on your own understanding.
In all your ways acknowledge him,
  and he will make your paths smooth.
Do not consider yourself wise.
Fear the LORD, and turn away from evil.
  ⌊Then⌋ your body will be healed,
    and your bones will have nourishment.

3:5-8

The fear of the LORD is the beginning of wisdom.
The knowledge of the Holy One is understanding.

9:10

The fear of the LORD lengthens ⌊the number of⌋ days,
  but the years of wicked people are shortened.

10:27

Whoever despises ⌊God's⌋ words will pay the penalty,
  but the one who fears ⌊God's⌋ commands will be rewarded.

13:13

Whoever lives right fears the LORD,
  but a person who is devious in his ways despises him.

14:2

Trusting God and the Fear of the Lord

In the fear of the LORD there is strong confidence,
and his children will have a place of refuge.
The fear of the LORD is a fountain of life
to turn ⌊one⌋ away from the grasp of death.

14:26-27

Better to have a little with the fear of the LORD
than great treasure and turmoil.

15:16

The fear of the LORD is discipline ⌊leading to⌋ wisdom,
and humility comes before honor.

15:33

Entrust your efforts to the LORD,
and your plans will succeed.

16:3

By mercy and faithfulness, peace is made with the LORD.
By the fear of the LORD, evil is avoided. . . .
Whoever gives attention to the LORD's word prospers,
and blessed is the person who trusts the LORD.

16:6,20

The name of the LORD is a strong tower.
A righteous person runs to it and is safe.

18:10

The fear of the LORD leads to life,
and such a person will rest easy without suffering harm.

19:23

Do not say, "I'll get even with you!"
Wait for the LORD, and he will save you.

20:22

On the heels of humility (the fear of the LORD)
  are riches and honor and life.

22:4

Open your ears, and hear the words of wise people,
  and set your mind on the knowledge I give you.
    It is pleasant if you keep them in mind
      ⌊so that⌋ they will be on the tip of your tongue,
      so that your trust may be in the LORD.
Today I have made them known to you, especially to you.
Didn't I write to you previously with advice and knowledge
  in order to teach you the words of truth
    so that you can give an accurate report
      to those who send you?

22:17-21

Do not envy sinners in your heart.
  Instead, continue to fear the LORD.
    There is indeed a future,
      and your hope will never be cut off.

My son,
  listen, be wise,
    and keep your mind going in the right direction.

23:17-19

Fear the LORD, my son.
Fear the king as well.
  Do not associate with those who always insist upon change,
    because disaster will come to them suddenly.
      Who knows what misery both may bring?

24:21-22

A greedy person stirs up a fight,
  but whoever trusts the LORD prospers.

Whoever trusts his own heart is a fool.
Whoever walks in wisdom will survive.

28:25-26

Trusting God and the Fear of the Lord

Without prophetic vision people run wild,
but blessed are those who follow ⌊God's⌋ teachings. . . .
A person's fear sets a trap ⌊for him⌋,
but one who trusts the LORD is safe.

29:18,25

Charm is deceptive, and beauty evaporates,
⌊but⌋ a woman who has the fear of the LORD
should be praised.

31:30

WOMEN AND MEN

Sometimes male and female perspectives of life can clash with each other. But both men and women can gain insight on relationships between each other and with God. These Proverbs advise us how.

Women and Men

A gracious woman wins respect,
  but ruthless men gain riches.

11:16

⌊Like⌋ a gold ring in a pig's snout,
  ⌊so⌋ is a beautiful woman who lacks good taste.

11:22

The wisest of women builds up her home,
  but a stupid one tears it down with her own hands.

14:1

Better to live on a corner of a roof
  than to share a home with a quarreling woman. . . .
Better to live in a desert
  than with a quarreling and angry woman.

21:9,19

Better to live on a corner of a roof
  than to share a home with a quarreling woman.

25:24

Constantly dripping water on a rainy day
    is like a quarreling woman.
  Whoever can control her can control the wind.
    He can even pick up olive oil with his right hand.

27:15-16

WRONG INFLUENCES AND CONTROLLING PEOPLE

Sometimes people try to lead us away from God. Through the Proverbs, God tells us we should not envy their wickedness. The verses in this section tell us to use God's gift of wisdom to scrutinize those influences and choose those with God-pleasing results.

Wrong Influences and Controlling People

My son,
if sinners lure you, do not go along.
If they say,
"Come with us.
Let's set an ambush to kill someone.
Let's hide to ambush innocent people for fun.
We'll swallow them alive like the grave,
like those in good health who go into the pit.
We'll find all kinds of valuable possessions.
We'll fill our homes with stolen goods.
Join us.
We'll split the loot equally."

My son,
do not follow them in their way.
Do not even set foot on their path,
because they rush to do evil
and hurry to shed blood.
It does no good to spread a net
within the sight of any bird.
But these people set an ambush for their own murder.
They go into hiding only to lose their lives.
This is what happens to everyone
who is greedy for unjust gain.
Greed takes away his life.

1:10-19

⌊Wisdom will⌋ save you
from the way of evil,
from the person who speaks devious things,
from those who abandon the paths of righteousness
to walk the ways of darkness,
from those who enjoy doing evil,
from those who find joy in the deviousness of evil.
Their paths are crooked.
Their ways are devious.

2:12-15

Do not envy a violent person.
Do not choose any of his ways.
The devious person is disgusting to the LORD.
The LORD's intimate advice is with decent people.

3:31-32

A wicked person delights in setting a trap for ⌞other⌟ evil people,
but the roots of righteous people produce ⌞fruit⌟.

12:12

Whoever walks with wise people will be wise,
but whoever associates with fools will suffer.

13:20

Stay away from a fool,
because you will not receive knowledge from his lips.

14:7

A violent person misleads his neighbor
and leads him on a path that is not good.

16:29

Drive out a mocker, and conflict will leave.
Quarreling and abuse will stop.

22:10

Do not be a friend of one who has a bad temper,
and never keep company with a hothead,
or you will learn his ways
and set a trap for yourself.

22:24-25

Do not associate with those who drink too much wine,
with those who eat too much meat,
because both a drunk and a glutton will become poor.
Drowsiness will dress a person in rags.

23:20-21

Wrong Influences and Controlling People

Do not envy evil people
  or wish you were with them,
    because their minds plot violence,
      and their lips talk trouble.

24:1-2

Fear the LORD, my son.
Fear the king as well.
  Do not associate with those who always insist upon change,
    because disaster will come to them suddenly.
      Who knows what misery both may bring?

24:21-22

Take the impurities out of silver,
  and a vessel is ready for the silversmith to mold.
Take a wicked person away from the presence of a king,
  and justice will make his throne secure.

25:4-5

⌊As⌋ iron sharpens iron,
  so one person sharpens the wits of another.

27:17

Whoever leads decent people into evil will fall into his own pit,
  but innocent people will inherit good things.

28:10

If a ruler pays attention to lies,
  all his servants become wicked.

29:12

Steps to Peace with God

God's Purpose: Peace and Life

God loves you and wants you to experience peace and life—abundant and eternal.

The Bible Says . . .

". . . we have peace with God through our Lord Jesus Christ." Romans 5:1

"For God so loved the world that He gave His only begotten Son, that whoever believes in Him should not perish but have everlasting life." John 3:16

". . . I have come that they may have life, and that they may have it more abundantly." John 10:10b

Since God planned for us to have peace and the abundant life right now, why are most people not having this experience?

Our Problem: Separation

God created us in His own image to have an abundant life. He did not make us as robots to automatically love and obey Him, but gave us a will and a freedom of choice.

We chose to disobey God and go our own willful way. We still make this choice today. This results in separation from God.

The Bible Says . . .

"For all have sinned and fall short of the glory of God." Romans 3:23

"For the wages of sin is death, but the gift of God is eternal life in Christ Jesus our Lord." Romans 6:23

Our choice results in separation from God.

Our Attempts

Through the ages, individuals have tried in many ways to bridge this gap . . . without success . . .

The Bible Says . . .

"There is a way that seems right to man, but in the end it leads to death." Proverbs 14:12

"But your iniquities have separated you from God; and your sins have hidden His face from you, so that He will not hear." Isaiah 59:2

There is only one remedy for this problem of separation.

Step 3 God's Remedy: The Cross

Jesus Christ is the only answer to this problem. He died on the Cross and rose from the grave, paying the penalty for our sin and bridging the gap between God and people.

The Bible Says . . .

". . . God is on one side and all the people on the other side, and Christ Jesus, Himself man, is between them to bring them together . . ." 1 Timothy 2:5

"For Christ also has suffered once for sins, the just for the unjust, that He might bring us to God . . ." 1 Peter 3:18a

"But God demonstrates His own love for us in this: While we were still sinners, Christ died for us." Romans 5:8

God has provided the only way . . . we must make the choice . . .

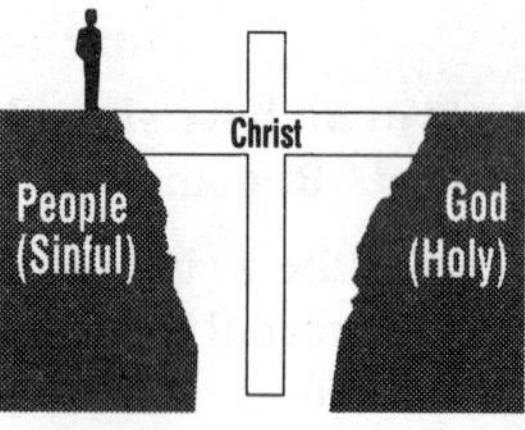

Our Response: Receive Christ

We must trust Jesus Christ and receive Him by personal invitation.

The Bible Says . . .

"Behold, I stand at the door and knock. If anyone hears My voice and opens the door, I will come in to him and dine with him, and he with Me." Revelation 3:20

"But as many as received Him, to them He gave the right to become children of God, even to those who believe in His name." John 1:12

". . . if you confess with your mouth the Lord Jesus and believe in your heart that God has raised Him from the dead, you will be saved." Romans 10:9

Are you here . . . or here?

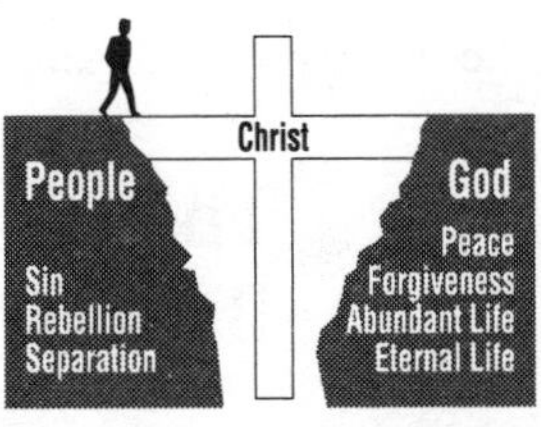

Is there any good reason why you cannot receive Jesus Christ right now?

How to receive Christ:

1. Admit your need (I am a sinner).
2. Be willing to turn from your sins (repent).
3. Believe that Jesus Christ died for you on the Cross and rose from the grave.
4. Through prayer, invite Jesus Christ to come in and control your life through the Holy Spirit. (Receive Him as Lord and Savior.)

What to Pray:

Dear Lord Jesus,

I know that I am a sinner and need Your forgiveness. I believe that You died for my sins. I want to turn from my sins. I now invite You to come into my heart and life. I want to trust and follow You as Lord and Savior.

In Jesus' name. Amen.

____________________ Date

____________________ Signature

God's Assurance: His Word

If you prayed this prayer,

The Bible Says...

"For 'whoever calls upon the name of the Lord will be saved.'" Romans 10:13

Did you sincerely ask Jesus Christ to come into your life? Where is He right now? What has He given you?

"For it is by grace you have been saved, through faith—and this is not from yourselves, it is the gift of God—not by works, so that no one can boast." Ephesians 2:8,9

The Bible Says...

"He who has the Son has life; he who does not have the Son of God does not have life. These things I have written to you who believe in the name of the Son of God, that you may know that you have eternal life, and that you may continue to believe in the name of the Son of God." 1 John 5:12–13, NKJV

Receiving Christ, we are born into God's family through the supernatural work of the Holy Spirit who indwells every believer...this is called regeneration or the "new birth."

This is just the beginning of a wonderful new life in Christ. To deepen this relationship you should:

1. Read your Bible every day to know Christ better.
2. Talk to God in prayer every day.
3. Tell others about Christ.
4. Worship, fellowship, and serve with other Christians in a church where Christ is preached.
5. As Christ's representative in a needy world, demonstrate your new life by your love and concern for others.

God bless you as you do.

Billy Graham

If you want further help in the decision you have made, write to:
Billy Graham Evangelistic Association P.O. Box 779, Minneapolis, Minnesota 55440-0779